for each dance, along with suggested musical selections, accompany the diagrams and photos. Dance and physical education teachers and students will find this section invaluable, and aspiring urban cowboys can follow the easy-to-read diagrammed footsteps to a satisfying spin around the honky-tonk floor. Anyone interested in dance or in the history of social customs in Texas will find much to enjoy in this refreshing and often amusing look at a Texas "national" pastime.

BETTY CASEY, author of *The Complete Book of Square Dancing (and Round Dancing)* and *International Folk Dancing, U.S.A.*, lives in Kerrville, Texas, where she continues to train dancers and to research and write about American traditional dancing.

DANCE ACROSS TEXAS

Dance across Texas

by BETTY CASEY

 UNIVERSITY OF TEXAS PRESS, AUSTIN

First Edition, 1985

Requests for permission to reproduce
material from this work should be sent
to Permissions, University of Texas
Press, Box 7819, Austin, Texas 78713.

LIBRARY OF CONGRESS CATALOGING
IN PUBLICATION DATA
Casey, Betty, 1916–
   Dance across Texas.
   Bibliography: p.
   Includes index.
   1. Dancing—Texas.   2. Country
   dance—Texas.
I. Title.
GV1624.T4C37   1985   793.3′4′09764
      84-24126
ISBN 0-292-71540-4

Contents

I lovingly dedicate this book to John, the helpful, congenial Texan with whom I have joyfully danced and taught these delightful dances—across Texas and around the world—since before our marriage in 1940.

Preface

Dancing was popular and lively in early Texas, as it is today. Part 1 of this book is packed with an informal collection of notes and anecdotes about the dances and the dancers—pioneer to present, rowdy and refined. There are descriptions of posh pioneer balls and cotillions directed by dancing masters, where ladies in elegant satin hoopskirts glided with gentlemen dressed in fashionable velvet jackets; and of informal get-togethers on isolated ranches where the dancers wore homespuns and buckskins, shared a pair of boots to dance in, and improvised the steps.

Accounts of the development and rise in popularity of country-western style music and the establishment of honkytonk dance halls show their influence on the increased interest in modernized versions of the old-time Texas dances. Descriptions of old and new dance clubs, honky-tonks, and popular dance halls pinpoint some of the places where Texans and their friends continue to dance across Texas.

Part 2 provides step-by-step instructions and illustrations for twenty-two authentic Texas dances that are living reminders of Texas' heritage. The easy-to-follow diagrams are unique in that they show the steps for partners simultaneously instead of separately.

As a native Texan, a longtime dancer and dance teacher, and the author of books on square dancing, round dancing, and folk dancing, writing this book has been gratifying to me in many respects. Through the years, several people have urged me to put Texas dances into a book, among them my son, Tom, and Dr. Charles Roth when he was president of Texas International Folk Dancers. Both pointed out that there was a real need for the dance instructions in the wake of the "country" dance mania across the nation, yet instructions for only a few of the dances were available. Part of my own motivation, however, was to record the dances lest they be lost.

The difficult part came after the University of Texas Press gave me the go-ahead on the book: I had then to decide which dances and which versions to include. The decisions were eventually made on the basis of suggestions from dance enthusiasts, popularity of the dances, space requirements, and my own preference.

Thus I commend to you the results of my efforts.

Acknowledgments

Much of the material in this book comes from a lifetime of dancing and teaching Texas dances. I thank the following people for their special contributions; however, I hold none of them in any way responsible for mistakes that might have been made.

For modeling: Gail and Eddie Sears, Walter and Maria Cracknell, Joy Neal, Patricia Phillips, James Michael Ross, Blaine and Ree Nelson, Marci Hunt, Tom Schmidt, Randy and Sandra Kelly, Ann Schladoer, Liz Dixon, Jennifer Dodson, Jim Teltschik, Larry Forrest, Heather Blankenship, Philip Cole Elam, Carl Spencer, Kari Scott, and Nathan Cox.

For interviews: Elaine Crider Hurt, for information on Crider's dance hall; Juanita Beasley, for the Cowboys' Christmas Ball; Hugo and Billie Real and Bella Schwethelm, for the German Club of Kerr County; Richard P. Corrigan and Marion A. Olson, Jr., for the San Antonio German Club; Lavinia Schlabach, for telling me about the double shuffle; Juan Tejada, for Mexican *conjunto* music; Garland Perry, Anhalt Hall, and Ross and Clarabelle Snodgrass, for the Garden Waltz.

For dance-diagram editing: Dot Hogan, Suzanne Slagle, William and Gladys Chamberlain, Lowell and Edra Bowdle, George and Marion Bakle, Charles and Kay Roth, Eldon and Marge Perry.

For proofreading: Karen Kemp, Ruth Sinex, Nina Ellis, Edra Bowdle, and John Casey.

For many tedious hours spent pasting frolicsome little footprints across the diagrams and for chauffering, assistance with research, general "gofering," and unstinting support: John B. Casey.

PART ONE
Background of Texas Dances

Overview of Texas Dancing

Early settlers arrived in the vast unsettled wilderness called Texas with dancing shoes ready. The immigrant peasantry introduced a variety of lusty folk dances, and high society took lessons from dancing masters and stepped out in refined European ballroom style—even before Texas won its independence from Mexico in 1836. In fact, an invitation was issued on July 19, 1832, in Brazoria to "a Public Dinner and Ball" honoring "the triumph of the cause of the Constitution and its distinguished advocate, General Santa Ana," who soon afterward became the archenemy of brash Texas independence seekers.

SANTA ANA DINNER AND BALL.

A PUBLIC DINNER AND BALL will be given at the Tavern of Thomas H. Brenen, on Saturday the 21st inst., in honor of the triumph of the cause of the Constitution and its distinguished advocate, General Santa Ana ; to which you are respectfully invited.

	Capt. Wiley Martin,
	Capt. John Austin,
	W. H. Wharton,
	W. J. Russell,
Brazoria, Thursday,	Luke Lesassier,
July 19, 1832.	J. Westall,
	D. W. Anthony,

Managers.

Courtesy Austin History Center (FP, D8, A2, Social Life and Customs), Austin, Texas.

The earliest settlers came mainly on ships from Germany, England, Ireland, France, or Spain; on horseback from Mexico; or by ship or jolting oxcart from eastern and southern states, where they had paused for a time after leaving the Old World. Along with their traditions, taste-tested recipes, and treasured heirlooms, they brought unique dance steps as reminders of faraway homelands and as a contribution to the culture of a developing new territory. And each batch of new arrivals brought the latest steps to liven up the dance scene.

Some people, wearing Sunday-best homespuns and crude boots, danced at isolated homes to which "everybody [was] invited, nobody slighted." They "stomped the splinters off of the split-log floors 'til daylight," or performed their jigs, schottisches, squares, and reels on wagon sheets spread on the ground.

Before Texas exchanged its status as a republic for statehood, many Texans were already celebrating July Fourth. For example, in 1838, the Veterans Association issued invitations requesting "the pleasure of your company" at a dinner and ball to be held in Velasco "in commemoration of the Independence of our Mother Land."

The socially elite in more populous areas received invitations bound in white satin. Dressed in the latest fashions of hooped silk gowns and velvet suits, they "postured and bowed in stately elegance" while dancing structured cotillions, germans, and quadrilles at posh formal balls.

Hospitality, gaiety, and dancing flourished at pioneer social events, such as barn raisings, quilting bees, weddings, military merrymaking, and holiday celebrations, despite the danger of Indian raids and the rigors of weather, pioneer life, and politics. The socials played an important part in the lives of the pioneers. They provided an opportunity for lonely, isolated settlers and bewildered newcomers to get acquainted and find much-needed companionship. They were the means in times before telephone, radio, and television of exchanging news and, more important, they made it possible for the unmarried to meet and for courtships to bloom.

The potpourri of nationalities with diverse economic backgrounds juggled jigsaw pieces of many cultures into a brash new state, at the same time creating a stalwart new breed of citizen, at first called Texian and later Texan. Meanwhile, their dances, none of which were indigenous to Texas, mixed and mingled congenially. They represented the mix of cultures stirred into the Texas mystique by people from many lands. Settlers hungry for social activities and ever ready to escape the monotony of long, harsh days spent taming a wide expanse of wilderness eagerly welcomed dances introduced by new arrivals. Where available, dancing masters taught the dance steps along with the social graces; more often, steps were learned by observing other dancers.

Changes occurred during this mingling of steps danced far from their origins. Just as traditions no longer relevant were replaced by new forms, and prized recipes had to be altered because of the unavailability of some ingredient, dance forms also adjusted to the new environment. Substitutions were made for some forgotten detail; new steps were designed to fit an old-time fiddler's different interpretation of a tune; and for diversion, two types of dance step and rhythm were combined and given a new name. Similar changes were all the while occurring in other states.

A fine mix of couple dances (sometimes called rounds) and structured group dances evolved. Schottisches, waltzes, mazurkas, jigs, polkas, lancers, quadrilles, cotillions, fandangos, square dances, and germans were danced at many affairs held by enthusiastic, social-minded Texans in the latter half of the 1800s. The September 1871 opening ball of the season in Austin included almost a dozen different titles, and a hop given by the Austin Dancing Club in 1883 included two types of waltz and three versions of lancer on its diverse program.

Around the turn of the century, frontier towns lost their isolation. Modern developments—radio, telephone, automobile, electricity—expanded their contact with the outside world. The car brought in touring musicians, minstrel shows, and entertainers. Small-town folk were treated to medicine shows, southern jazz, and the latest trends in dance steps. Life speeded up as the century turned; new music and dance steps with more standard forms swept like a prairie fire across the wide open spaces of Texas, pushing the old traditional steps aside. Just after the turn of the century, in fact, Texas dance cards (as evidenced by the Elks Club dance card of September 9, 1913) showed only a monotonous alter-

Opening Ball of the Season.
❦❦❦
Programme.

1. March, *Willowdale*..........................
2. Quadrille....................................
3. Waltz, *"Nobody's Darling"*..................
4. Polka, *"Tremolo"*..........................
5. Lancers.....................................
6. Redowa......................................
7. Varsouvienne................................
8. Quadrille....................................
9. Kiss Waltz..................................
0. Schottische, *'Silver Cloud"*...............
1. Camille.....................................
2. Lancers.....................................
3. Polka Redowa................................
4. Galop, *"Carlotta"*.........................
5. Quadrille....................................
6. Waltz, *"Ristori"*..........................
7. Fling Schottische...........................
8. Mazourka, *"Twilight Thoughts"*.............

Opening Ball of the Season,
AT THE
Raymond House,
Wednesday Evening, September 20, 1871.

Committee of Invitation.

Hon. W. H. PYLE.	Col. J. O. TRACY.
Hon. J. S. MILLS.	Hon. T. J. CHAMBERS.
Hon. J. P. DOUGLAS.	Hon. IRA H. EVANS.
Hon. W. A. BAYLOR.	Capt. F. L. BRITTON.

The presence of yourself and ladies is respectfully solicited.

Dr J Watkins

Courtesy Austin History Center (U4500, Social Life and Customs), Austin, Texas.

nation of the waltz and the two-step. Yet some versions of pioneer dances were preserved in scattered pockets in the hills and on the prairies of the state by people dedicated to enjoying the dances that are authentic witness to the life of early Texans.

During the ensuing years, Texas joined the national zoo parade in the antics of the Grizzly Bear, the Bunny Hug, and the equally grotesque Texas Tommy. These were soon replaced by other dances set to a greater variety of music. Ragtime, blues, jazz, and Latin beats spawned the Charleston, blackbottom, one-step, fox-trot, tango, cha-cha-cha, and a host of others.

For the elite, the Lindy Hop, jitterbug, and slow dancing rolled into the state in the 1930s accompanied by the big bands—Dorsey, Miller, Welk, Garber, Brown, King, Waring, Weems, Lombardo. Local bands and jukeboxes at the honky-tonks kept the beer drinkers in step to the same rhythms, with an occasional schottische added for old times' sake.

After World War II a strange phenomenon occurred. Suddenly it seemed that everyone in the nation wanted to learn the old-fashioned square dance, and the movement grew to fad proportions. No one knows exactly why. Perhaps it was because, as hostilities phased out, war-weary, fun-hungry people were eager to make new friends and develop new recreational skills, to relax and laugh again. Returning servicemen reunited with wives and sweethearts in their hometowns—deep in mountain hollows, high on windswept plains, and in the lowlands along sandy seashores—discovered the refreshing charisma of the early dances. And Texas was ready to take part in the revival. Dr. Lloyd "Pappy" Shaw of Colorado did much of his research in Texas for his books *Cowboy Dances* and *The Round Dance Book*. He discovered and recorded dances that had never died at all; they had only been in hiding.

Existing square dance groups expanded, new "callers" developed, and new groups were formed. Their programs included the early couple dances—schottische, polka, waltz, Put Your Little Foot, and two-step. Costumes fashioned after those earlier days featured hooped skirts, western shirts, and neckerchiefs.

Soon, however, the old-time "watch me and learn" square dance routines were replaced by newly invented and more complicated patterns. This embellishment developed nationwide into a unique American dance form based on the classic four-couple square formation of the quadrille. Popular tunes were added to the old standbys and used as background for the extemporaneous calling out of a plethora of movements by a caller. The American square dance acquired its own identity.

The simple steps of the classic couple dances also underwent many changes and utilized ever-expanding numbers of routines set to rhythms ranging from rhumba to swing. The new couple dances, which became known as round dances, required exacting choreography performed simultaneously by couples following each other around a large circle.

The development of public-address systems, record players, and microphones, and the appearance of special records for square and round dances made it possible for larger and larger groups to dance to one square dance caller or one round dance prompter. Soon, square dancers and round dancers developed firmly established, separate programs based on clubs. Membership and participation in either group required courses of instruction and costumes adjusted to more comfortable, modern attire featuring shorter skirts over bouncy petticoats for women and western attire for men. Both groups had large followings in the 1980s. (See my *The Complete Book of Square Dancing [and Round Dancing]* for more details.) In 1982, Congress officially proclaimed the square dance the "national folk dance." Again, the easy, early couple dances went underground, to be kept on hold by a few Texas clubs and country-western dance halls.

Other fads had followed the square dance phenomenon. A type of dance emerged from the rebellion during the late 1940s against restrictions of standard social couple-dance patterns. In the twist dancers improvised solo steps to jive or rock 'n' roll rhythms; discotheques introduced the Frug and the Chicken. Standardization eventually crept into some dances and nontouching dancers formed drill lines across the floor in such dances as Four Corners, or couples choreographed elaborate dances performed under colored strobe lights to thunderous music.

Another national phenomenon occurred in the 1970s and 1980s. The simple tried-and-true waltzes, schottisches, and other dance steps enjoyed by the first Texans, but put aside for many years, emerged into the spotlight under the name of "country-western," "cowboy," or plain "country" dances (the last tied in with the burgeoning popularity of "country music," not with an identity as rural dances). A *Redbook* magazine article stated, "The whole damn country is going Texan." The *Wall Street Journal* headlined, "Country Western Dance Halls Spring Up As Discos Fade." Dancers nationwide even dressed the part in cowboy boots, hats, and jeans.

To accommodate the singles in attendance, creative Texans resurrected old nonpartner, spoke-line dances and in-

Abilene Lifters Dance Group demonstrates 1950s-style dancing at the state Capitol in 1976; Betty and John Casey are the dancers at far right. Fredrick Photos, Austin, Texas.

vented new ones. They changed some of the formations from couple to spoke-lines and altered the steps to fit, so that lines made up of happy single dancers could link arms around each other's waists and prance or glide happily around the hall. Country music dance band programs showed a mix of schottische, polka, Cotton-eyed Joe hoedown, and Put Your Little Foot music with a touch of Bob Wills' western swing and the latest danceable Barbara Mandrell, Willie Nelson, or Mickey Gilley two-step or waltz. Dancers across the nation welcomed the new style with open arms.

There are various speculations on the reason for this development. It is sometimes attributed to a culmination of forces that had begun to gather long before. A major contributing factor was the development and promotion of country- and western-style music, musicians, and movies. Another theory proposed that a nation immersed in deafening music and disco gyrations and lifestyles, hemmed in by big business and computerized boundaries, suddenly discovered an es-cape in danceable music, easy-to-learn dance steps, and comfortable clothing. Cowboy hats and boots, calico, and blue jeans became the order of the day. Aaron Latham, co-screenwriter of the 1980 movie *Urban Cowboy*, said when interviewed by the *Wall Street Journal*, "As the country grows more complex it seems to need simpler and simpler values—something like the cowboy code."

At any rate, a down-home country flavor infiltrated the modern world on every level, and the Texas cowboy image and Texas couple and spoke-line dances spread from the Atlantic to the Pacific in the 1980s.

Texas dances are a living bit of the colorful days of the Old West. Beaten out by trial and error in the crude forge of happenstance, they are fashioned from fragments of dances brought as part of the cultural baggage of early settlers from many places.

The dances that have evolved are lively and vibrantly danceable; the steps are uncomplicated and easy to do. These dances are what *Dance across Texas* is all about.

2

Early Texas Dancing

Social gatherings held for the purpose of doing different types of dancing, from early American and early Texas days to the present, have been called by an odd mixture of names often used interchangeably: balls, cotillions, germans, hops, and fandangos. The names in Texas reflect the influence of diverse cultures accompanying the adventurous people who were attracted by free land and opportunity. At times the name indicated the exact nature of the dancing actually done at the affair described, but quite often the name had no connection with the program of dances offered. Originally, at a cotillion the cotillion was danced; at a german the german was danced. When new dances were introduced, or when several types of dance appeared on the same program, or perhaps when the original dance was dropped entirely, the original name for a dance social or club might be retained.

BALLS

The present-day American use of the word *ball* to describe a large, formal gathering for social dancing derives from the French word *bal*, meaning an assembly for the purpose of dancing. Some occasions fit this description, but there was nothing formal or even large about other so-called balls in pioneer times. In fact, a small, informal dance held in a home where only square dancing was done was sometimes described as a ball.

At Mrs. Long's boarding house in Houston in 1835, for example, "the colonists held an elaborate dinner and ball" honoring Stephen F. Austin, "with one thousand colonists in attendance." Another account describes a jig done at a "fancy dress ball" held in a "one room log cabin" where they "moved beds and other furniture out into the prairie that extended about 345 miles" from the house. At Houston in 1837, "settlers came in wagons and on horseback, bringing their best clothes to wear to celebrate the great victory [of the battle of San Jacinto] at a grand ball. . . . The courthouse was ablaze with candles as reels were called to the music of a single violin."

At the 1883 inaugural ball for John Ireland, held in the temporary capitol in Austin, "over 2500 people thronged the hall and passages." At an Austin ball held in 1841, "the cotillion, the waltz and the promenade . . . proceeded . . . to the slow time of a warlike air." The climax of commencement week at the University of Texas before 1900 was the Final Ball, always held on the second floor of the Driskill Hotel. In San Antonio, "grand balls" were held at the Menger Hotel and the San Antonio Club above the Grand Opera House on Alamo Plaza. A New Year's ball was held in 1899 at the Matzdorf Hotel in New Braunfels.

The March 19, 1886, issue of the *Taylor County News* published a typical program of a western ball. It included twenty dances with descriptive names, such as Grand Circle Round-Up; Fourth Guard Quadrilles; Catch-Horse and Day-Herder's Waltz; Bronco and Cow-and-Calf Racquet, Circular Gallop; Round-Up and Night-Horse Lancers; and Maverick's Polka. It concluded with Stampede All.

COTILLIONS

Some dance socials were, and are, called "cotillions." The word is an Americanized version of the name *cotillon*, a French quadrille dance brought to America by early settlers. The French word means "petticoat" and comes from the lyrics to a song to which the quadrille was danced: "Ma commere, quand je

New Year's Ball, 1899, at the Matzdorf Hotel in New Braunfels; white dresses were the latest fashion. Courtesy Sophienburg Memorial Association, New Braunfels.

danse mon cotillon va-t-il bien?" ("My dear, when I dance does my petticoat go well?"). The cotillion, danced by four couples forming a square, had so many complicated figures it required instruction from a dancing master. (Some of the cotillion figures and steps are described briefly in the section "Dances and Dancing Masters.") Today, cotillions are thought of as formal dances at which freestyle standard couple dancing is done.

Many dance socials were called cotillions by early Texas settlers. In December 1856, for example, an announcement was published in Austin of "a cotillion party . . . to come off at Peck's new store . . . in preparation for the holidays." In 1895 "the cotillion at the Driskill [Hotel] last night, under the auspices of the Capital City Cotillion Club, was one of those brilliant . . . affairs. . . . The

wealth, youth, beauty and culture of Texas were present."

GERMANS

Other dance parties were once called "germans," and some dance clubs throughout the country still operate under the name German Club. This name does not necessarily indicate any relationship to Germany or its people. The german, a French dance no longer in vogue, was part of the cultural contribution of early-day dancing masters.

The French word *german* means "a family member." The dance was called a german, according to C. H. Cleveland, Jr., in his book *Dancing at Home and Abroad*, "because of its neighborly or family character." It was performed in a circle with no set number of couples and consisted of many intricate figures directed by a floor manager or director who had taken instruction from a dancing master. (Some of the many figures of the german are described briefly in the section "Dances and Dancing Masters.")

Originally, at dancing parties called germans early settlers performed the german. Later, as the complicated figures were replaced by other, newer, freestyle couple dances, such as the polka and waltz, the dances changed, but the name for the occasion was retained for many years. Also, at some dances called "hops," the german was included on the program with such other dances as the waltz and lancers.

At the same time as newer dances were replacing the german, many private dance clubs where the german was not danced were organized under the name German Club. Again, although the set formations of the old dance known as the german lost favor and it was dropped in favor of simpler dances, many clubs retained the name of German Club.

Many germans were written up in Austin papers after the state capital was moved there from Houston. In 1887 a "round of gaiety led off . . . with a regular 'meet' of the Austin German Club at Washington Fire Company's new hall," and "on Friday evening a german will be given at the residence of one of Austin's most popular belles." "With three german clubs organized and ready for active pleasure, the social season . . . promises to be exceptionally bright."

"The first german of the season, to be given by the Capital German Club," was announced in October 1889. "This will doubtless usher in the long series of germans. . . . The Capital German Club is composed of about twenty young men who have in the past been noted for the excellency of their entertainments."

The University of Texas, established in 1883, held frequent dances. Some were billed as balls, and some as germans and cotillions, even after those two dances were dropped from the programs. Activi-

ties at commencements before 1900 "began with a 'morning German' at 6:30 A.M. aboard the riverboat Ben Hur which carried 2,000 passengers. At these Germans a cotillion leader would call figures (marching, dividing, etc.). Sometimes couples would dance a waltz between figures."

HOPS

Dance socials have been called "hops" since the 1700s. In 1730 the word was defined as "slang for an informal dance." Reed's *Weekly Journal* mentioned "a three-penney hop" attended by a hundred people, and Jane Austen wrote of an event that happened "at a little hop." It

Courtesy Austin History Center (S3106, Social Life and Customs), Austin, Texas.

Old-time ball reenactment, 1925, by West Texas State Teacher's College students. Courtesy Panhandle-Plains Historical Museum, Canyon, Texas.

has been a general name for dance socials incorporating a mixture of dances.

Many hops were held by the first settlers in Texas, especially at Austin, a very social-minded town. In December 1874 a newspaper described "the first social hop . . . given at the Raymond house" as "one of the most pleasant affairs." At the hop, "the social opened with a grand march . . . and the light streamed down on Austin's fairest daughters as they whirled through the mazy waltz or moved in stately style amid the figures of the plain quadrille, and with elegant grace to the music of the lancers or the charming waltz quadrille." After supper, "the german was introduced."

FANDANGOS

Dancing has always been an important feature of Mexican life, in Mexico and among early settlers from that country in Texas. The old name for a Mexican dance gathering was *fandango*, a name quite familiar to many Texas pioneers, especially in the southern part of the state.

At fandangos, they danced *bailes*, spirited couple dances derived from Spanish couple dances; *danzas*, group dances telling a story; and many European

dances introduced into Mexico when the Hapsburg Maximilian sat on the throne of that country. Mexican dances introduced into Texas included the Jarabe Tapatío (Mexican Hat Dance), *la jota*, *el fandango*, waltz, polka, Put Your Little Foot, *redova* (two-step), and quadrilles. They were performed with much flair and foot stamping. Among the Mexicans in Texas, there were rowdy public fandangos "patronized by the lower classes" and elegant private affairs, diligently chaperoned by older women. Fandangos added a bright note to the arduous, often dull and dreary lives of many Texas settlers of other ethnic origins.

In 1850, when more than half of the five thousand population of San Antonio was Mexican, democratic "good fellowship prevailed" at community entertainments, such as "Sunday horse races, cock fights, fandangos (dances) and the celebration of Saints' Days." Festivities in honor of saints' days were held June 24 through June 29, signaling the opening of the fruit and vegetable season, and ". . . each night a grand ball was held."

In 1856 a lieutenant stationed at Fort Bliss near El Paso recorded that "life at the post was dull enough until the fiestas commenced, then bullfights, . . .

The fandango, *Frank Leslie's Illustrated Newspaper*, January 15, 1859. Courtesy Library of the Daughters of the Republic of Texas at the Alamo, San Antonio, Texas.

bailes . . . and intrigue . . . made gay and noisy scenes where but an hour before all was as monotonous as the desert."

Frank Leslie's Illustrated Newspaper contained the following vivid description of dancing in San Antonio in 1859:

> Mexican amusements, . . . cock-fights, and fandangoes, help elevate and refine the people of San Antonio. . . . At these fandangoes may be seen the muleteer, fresh from the coast or the pass, with gay clothes and a dozen or so silver dollars; the United States soldiers just from the barracks, abounding in oath and tobacco; the herdsman, with his blanket and the long knife, which seems to be a portion of every Mexican; the disbanded ranger, rough, bearded and armed with his huge holster pistol and long bowie knife, dancing, eating, drinking, swearing and carousing, like a party of Captain Kidd's men just in from a long voyage.

In contrast to this informal scene, in the Palace of the Governors in San Antonio the official families of the various governments of Spain and Mexico held stately functions. There "the ladies were richly and extravagantly attired."

Dance Programs

Essentially, two types of dance social were in vogue during Texas' brash, adventuresome frontier era: large, formal, invitational affairs that "respectfully solicit your company" were organized in the towns, usually by young men's clubs, for the socially elite; and smaller, informal, "all invited, none slighted" open dances that included children were staged by the unsophisticated in less-populated areas. There were both subscription dances, where everyone paid to attend, and complimentary dances financed by some group or host. Nevertheless, for all types of gathering, sacrosanct codes of behavior were ensured by eagle-eyed floor managers, who not only made out the schedule of dances but also controlled exuberance, enforced courtesy and good taste, and arranged the pairing of dancers.

Formal invitations included a dance card with a numbered list of the dances to be offered on the program. Couples usually began the dance with a grand march, after which the lady's escort would mark several dances on her card for himself, including the good-night waltz. Then he would get other men to sign up for the remaining dances, at the same time marking their own cards beside corresponding numbers and thus committing themselves to "having the pleasure of" each other's company for that dance. A lady who didn't get her card filled was considered a wallflower.

The cards themselves were often works of art and were prized as souvenirs. With covers ranging from white satin to leather or colored paper with engraved or printed pictures and slogans, they were accompanied by tiny pencils tied on with bright ribbons or tasseled silk cords. In addition to the name of the occasion, the date and place, the names of illustrious personages serving as managers and on arrangement and reception committees were also listed.

At informal dances, often held in isolated homes with limited space, instead of using separate dance cards, the floor managers took charge. Since all could not dance at once, they made lists of the men, who usually outnumbered the women, and the ladies the men chose for each dance, then told them when it was their turn to "bow to a partner."

Dances and Dancing Masters

No pastime in American history has been indulged in with more gusto or seriousness than dancing on the frontier. As a Texas woman explained, "Times were too pregnant with excitement for grave pleasures to take strong hold of the minds of the people. . . . How could people sit often to listen to grave discourses when at every random shot of a gun their ears were on the alert for the cry of Indians. . . . It predisposes the mind to seek relief in softer emotions of pleasure, but still one of excitement." In *Dancing at Home and Abroad*, an instruction book written in Galveston in 1877, C. H. Cleveland, Jr., one of a number of dancing masters in Texas, stated his case: "I consider dancing not the least among the fine arts . . . that a knowledge of dancing with its collateral advantages should be acquired by those who are qualified with taste, intelligence, and means, just as necessarily as music, painting, poetry, sculpture, and letters. . . . Therefore I address myself to that element in society composed of people with liberal and comprehensive minds, quick and courteous sensibilities, and artistic tastes."

Dance teachers made it clear that at dances partners should be properly introduced, no profane language would be tolerated, and boys would wear coats and not tuck pants into boots and should hold a white or silk handkerchief in the right hand at their partners' waists to avoid soiling their dresses with perspiration. C. H. Cleveland, in fact, pronounced the man's "first and most necessary qualification" to be the "knowledge how to support, sustain and guide the lady in her movements. . . . He should understand the engineering of *trains* in all their most extravagant curves, lengths and contortions." At dancing schools in San Antonio, early Texans learned "the social graces" and how to do "such dances as the lanciers, the polka, the quadrille, and the waltz."

In 1839 J. R. Codet of New York opened the "Dancing and Waltzing Academy" in Houston. Soon afterward, an advertisement announced that "Mr. Arignon begs leave to inform the public . . . that he has engaged the Saloon at the Exchange Hotel, for the purpose of giving lessons in Dancing, Teaching waltzing, and all the most fashionable dances now in vogue in Europe. . . . There will be given Cotillion parties every Friday evening. . . . A good orchestra in attendance on the nights of the balls." He charged one dollar for lessons in cotillions and reels.

The Cotton and Stigler families dominated the dance instruction scene in Galveston from 1857 until the beginning of the Civil War. They were also professional musicians and "promoted private balls and cotillions." Professor Cotton's pupils gave a complimentary party for him in 1857 at which "the most popular dances of the day were scheduled—quadrilles, cotillions, mazurkas, schottisches, galopades, waltzes and polkas."

Fraternal organizations had special dances. The Sons of Temperance had balls regularly from 1849. "Balls were given for bachelors, fire companies, and military drill companies—The Washington Light Guard and The Houston Light Guard. The organization of germans, The Turnverein, sponsored an annual ball in January of each year after 1858 which was the highlight of the after-Christmas social calendar."

In the late 1800s Professor Whitehead and his son Rufus, who were also proficient fiddlers, went about the state giving lessons in round (couple) dancing and ballroom etiquette. During a two-week summer course held in Cherokee County, with afternoon and evening classes, they added the waltz, schottische, and polka to the square dancing already in vogue there. In a beautiful pecan grove, the young men of Cherokee built a "commodious" dancing platform of good, smooth lumber and provided "comfortable seats with backs for the dancers and the onlookers." Some two dozen boys and girls from San Saba and Cherokee attended. At a charge of five dollars each, the take was not bad for those days.

Some of the dances that appeared on fancy dance cards and were depicted in accounts of the informal balls handled by managers or directors enjoyed only

brief popularity before being relegated to the discard heap of history; a few are still around in one form or another. Those that remain have been molded and shaped by the setting and the stamp of bold characteristics they display into unique forms that Texans claim as their own.

Early dance steps fell into categories of couple- and group-dance formations, with an occasional jig performed solo. The group dances (those danced by more than two persons) were performed in various formations: facing lines, circles, and squares. In a later development, some of the couple-dance steps were choreographed for performance in single-line formation, placing them in both the couple and group categories.

COUPLE DANCES

Couple dances included waltzes, mazurkas, minuets, varsouvianas (Put Your Little Foot), two-steps, polkas, and schottisches. In the very earliest days, when women wore trains, the man had to dance backward with the lady following, in order not to step on the trailing material. After dress styles eliminated trains, it became customary for the men to dance forward so they could see where they were going and head off collisions. This change in dress style also made it possible to introduce many new dance variations.

Minuet. The colonial minuet was a stately couple dance performed in slow wedding-march cadence and accompanied by deep bows and much posturing, always at arm's length. The bows (curtsies for the ladies) were done carefully in order not to displace the men's powdered wigs and the ladies' high, exaggerated coiffures. It was one of the dances that the waltz replaced.

Waltz. The popular waltz, danced to three-count rhythms in closed position, took various forms under different names. It began as a fast, dizzying, exuberant couple dance characterized by constant hopping and turning. The origin of this dance from the 1700s is much debated in Europe, but there is no denying the influence of the lilting, melodic Strauss waltzes, which swept the dizzying, turning waltz steps into the dance halls of France and Germany. England succumbed to the leaping, whirling steps danced by couples holding each other in close embrace; then it crossed the Atlantic. It was popular even on frontier Texas dance floors. In the early 1900s, pretty Irene Castle cast aside restrictive corsets and high pompadours for free-flowing dresses and bobbed hair, and with her husband, Vernon, she led the nation into a new style of ballroom dancing.

Because of Texas' warm climate (no air conditioning then) and the resulting drain on vitality, Texans soon interspersed slower-paced versions into the programs. The pursuit waltz, danced around the floor without turning, retained its vigor with leaps on alternating feet on the first step of each measure.

The racquet (racket) waltz had many variations. In a basic pattern the first step forward was held for the first two beats of the measure, followed by a quick closing of the trailing foot with "a little undercut" and stepping in place with the lead foot, both steps taken on the third beat.

The Boston (glide) waltz is described by C. H. Cleveland, Jr., in *Dancing at Home and Abroad*. A quote credited to Dodworth, a prominent dancing master, reads, "We had been hopping in the 'hop waltz,' jumping in the quick 'redowa,' . . . had allowed those who were so inclined free license to tear about in a galop, until this desire for a change to a more composed and gentle style became general. This manifested itself first in subduing the 'redowa,' and . . . resulted in the present 'Boston.' . . . It now approaches that beautiful old-fashioned dance, the Spanish waltz."

Instructions for the Boston included the following:

> Heels together; toes turned out.
> LADY
> Step forward with the *right* foot eighteen inches; and in making this step bend the *left* knee, but keep the
> 1. right leg straight, allowing the *heel* to touch the floor an instant before the toes. (This bending of the left knee causes a descent of the body, from which the name dip is derived.)
> Pass the left beyond the right foot about eighteen inches, at the same time stiffening both legs and rising
> 2. (slightly) on the toes; while thus passing the left foot, turn nearly half round toward the right hand.
> Bring right heel against left heel,
> 3. settling down upon both, and thus finish the half turn.

The "rise" and "settling down" described in numbers two and three were still practiced by Texas old-timers in 1983.

There were many steps to the ländler waltz, so named for the Landl mountain region in Austria. It included numerous one-hand twirls of the lady, with her bouffant skirts flying, followed by vigorous turning steps in closed position.

The lovely old-time European waltz routine, now popularly called Put Your Little Foot, began as a mazurka step in the 1800s and has been known by several names. It has been called Little Foot and New Shoes, because those words are included in the lyrics to the "Put Your Little Foot" song. A more formal name, varsovienne (varsouviana) is thought by some to stem from the belief that the dance originated in Poland, where it was very popular; the name derives from Warsaw (with the first *W* pronounced *V*, as is the custom there).

Some special dance tunes combining an alternating mixture of a few measures of three-count waltz music with a few measures of four-count polka music be- came popular just after the turn of the century. Although containing polka steps, these combinations were called waltzes and have specific dance-step rou- tines. One such dance is called the Rye Waltz and another the Garden Waltz. Per- haps they were devised by a playful mu- sician to liven up a dull evening or to surprise the dancers with sudden changes in rhythm.

The waltz step has remained a favor- ite on Texas dance floors and has been adapted to many patterns. In couple combinations it is danced forward, back- ward, in a box pattern, with dips, twirls, and turns.

With the rise in popularity of unpart- nered, spoke-line dances, such as Cotton- eyed Joe and schottische, it seemed to me that there should be a waltz pattern that could be done in a line. Therefore, I wrote one (published for the first time in Part 2 of this book). Although it may be danced to any waltz music, it goes espe- cially well with "Waltz across Texas," an old Texas favorite. It may also be danced by a couple in open position, using a shoulder (varsouviana) hold.

Two-Step. The two-step is another step with roots in European and Mexi- can dance history. The step, danced by couples, appeared in the 1800s in Ger- many and Hungary and, most surely, the similar steps danced at Mexican fandan- gos left their influence in Texas. The step continues to be popular on Texas dance floors both as an integral part of dance routines, such as Cotton-eyed Joe and Cowboy Polka, and as a basic step used in freestyle couple dancing.

Early names for some types of two- step, often accompanied by prancing leaps or playful skips, were deux-temps, redowa, and galop. The name two-step no doubt derives from the fact that, al- though three steps are taken, the dancer progresses only two steps. The galop, not a true two-step, is now called a side-

close step, as in the dance Herr Schmidt, which is still popular in some areas. It is an energetic dance similar to many de- scribed in older European dance books. It has a routine set to the tune "Herr Schmidt" ("Mr. Smith"), which infers that it is of German origin. Deux-temps was a two-step done to waltz rhythm and has been called "the ignoramus waltz."

The double shuffle is an early-day type of two-step, still popular and danced al- most in one spot, shifting only slightly to alternating sides. "I learned it from my uncle," said a gray-haired woman, "when I was only belt-buckle high to him." "My brother and I put a Charleston twist on it to ragtime rhythm," recalled another grandmother.

Polka. It is believed that the polka originated in 1830 as a hippity-hop half- step designed by Anna Slezak, a little Bohemian peasant girl, to a tune she had made up. Joseph Neruda, her school- master, saw the dance, wrote it down, and taught it to his students. It was catchy so it became popular. In 1840 a dancing master in Prague took it for ex- hibition in Paris, and from there it found its way into European dancing salons and, eventually, to America. The name comes from the Bohemian word *pulka*, which means half-step.

At one time the polka was such a fa- vorite step in Europe and America that dancing masters invented numerous in- novations, such as side-step glides or galops, to combine with it. The once- popular Esmeralda Polka, included on many old dance programs, included three side-step glides.

A side-step galop polka routine that is still popular at many Texas dances is called the Seven-Step Polka, the name having derived from the German tune "Siebenschritt." The polka has been es- pecially popular among people of central European background.

Polkas have always abounded on Texas dance floors, sometimes taking a name related to the step pattern danced, such as heel-and-toe polka, and sometimes being called by the name of the tune to which they are danced most frequently, such as Little Brown Jug and Cotton-eyed Joe. There have been other early polkas called Bohemian, Saratoga, and Esmeralda. I have been unable to find descriptions of the first two.

Couples in many areas continue to enjoy the vigorous, hopping polka steps, but the Texas version is usually done as a spirited two-step without the hop—perhaps in deference to heavy cowboy boots or perhaps because the warmer climate is less invigorating than that of the country of origin.

The dance now called Cowboy Polka was choreographed for round dancing to a catchy Mexican polka tune, "Jesuscita in Chihuahua," Americanized as "Jessie Polka." In the 1970s and 1980s country-western dancers revised it and adopted it. They changed the position into a nonpartnered spoke-line using a waist hold, and now dance the routine to any polka tune.

The Cotton-eyed Joe, a lively, all-time favorite Texas dance, which is performed both as a couple dance and as a single-line group dance, is danced to a tune by the same name (on occasion called "the South Texas National Anthem"). It is an adapted polka considered to be a true Texas dance. Originally played for minstrel-type jigs, it is thought to have originated on the "wrong side of the tracks." It has long been popular as a square dance hoedown and a couple-dance polka and was a favorite for social dancing when played in swing time by Bob Wills.

Al Dean, leader of a country-western band, recalls hearing the tune called "The Gingerbread Boy" in South Texas. After he recorded an instrumental version as "Cotton-eyed Joe" in 1967, a new round-dance polka for couples was written for it. Country-western dancers discovered this dance and adapted a

simplified version of it to a nonpartner, waist-hold, spoke-line routine. They replaced the heel-and-toe polka steps with a cross-lift followed by a kick combined with two-steps. The lift and kick are sometimes accompanied by shouts of "whoops, whoops," and sometimes by a barnyard term, "bull shit," signifying the act of kicking off barnyard muck.

During the 1980s, this line version gained popularity not only on Texas dance floors but also across the nation and even in foreign countries. In it, lines of people in spoke-line formations move forward and backward like a gigantic wheel turning on its side around the dance floor. In Texas Hill Country styling the cross-lift and kick-step are smoothly controlled. One cowgirl told me, "If you can raise your boot up high, your jeans aren't tight enough."

Conjunto. During the 1930s and 1940s, another significant and very danceable type of music evolved in Mexico and swept across the border into Texas. It is known as *música norteña* in Mexico and *conjunto* music in Texas. *Conjunto* bands include an accordion and an adapted twelve-string bass guitar and drums. The music features spirited polka and two-step, four-count rhythms with a strong beat, all borrowed and adapted from German polka music and dance. The steps danced by couples to Mexican polkas, and the dance positions and holds used, demonstrate great individuality. Some of the steps are borrowed from a Mexican folk dance called the *corrida*, also known as "Eso Sí, Como No."

Schottische. The schottische is one of the oldest of all couple dances. The basic pattern, step-step-step-hop, is thought by some to have originated in Poland, although the dictionary indicates that the word *schottische* comes from the German word for Scottish. An encyclopedia states flatly that the dance was created at Markowski's dancing academy in 1850.

At any rate, practically every country

in the world includes the enjoyable step in at least one of its folk dances. There are many variations under numerous names. Some of these as danced in Texas are the Barn Dance, Military Schottische, Horse and Buggy, Belen, Bluebonnet, Drisken, the Highland, and Ten Pretty Girls. Ten Pretty Girls has a side-step schottische in it and is danced to the tune by the same name. A popular spoke-line version of the schottische, as done in Texas, is another example of an old-time couple dance revised into line formation and adopted by today's country music and dance lovers.

One-Step. The one-step, danced either in couple or line formation, is as easy as striding across a prairie. Beginning dancers can do it the first time they try. It requires simply stepping evenly, taking one step after another, either forward, backward, or turning, as in walking. In fact, in dance directions it is often called "walk." For example, "Walk four steps."

Shuffle Step. The shuffle step is probably the most popular dance step for

couples on Texas dance floors. The term "shuffle" refers to the smooth shuffling styling of the step, danced with feet close to the floor to country music. The step has even been erroneously called the "Texas two-step" and the "three-step."

Originally called a foxtrot, the versatile step has been a favorite, using several different styles, since it was devised by dancer-comedian Harry Fox for the Ziegfeld Follies review in 1913. Although it began with bouncy styling to go with the developing syncopation of jazz blues music of the times, the steps were gradually standardized by Vernon and Irene Castle, and it has remained popular everywhere since then.

Swing Step. Although not strictly based on old-time dance steps, the infectious syncopated western swing step, similar to the jitterbug, rock 'n' roll, and the Lindy Hop, evolved from a combination of factors that established it in the country music and dance scene. The big band sound of the 1940s incorporated

People crowding around the bandstand at a Bob Wills dance in California during World War II, probably early 1944. Courtesy Charles R. Townsend, *San Antonio Rose: The Life and Music of Bob Wills* (Urbana: University of Illinois Press, 1976).

jazz, blues, and ragtime syncopation into popular foxtrot tunes that evolved into a new sound—swing.

Native Texan Bob Wills and his Texas Playboys created a western swing rhythm characterized by a strong, insistent beat, jazzlike improvisations on the steel guitar, and a heavily bowed fiddle. Swing was, and is, catchy music designed for dancing, and the swing step was developed to accompany it.

There is wide variation in the number of spins and turns in the dance, yet some dancers are content to just flex their knees on the downbeat in accompaniment to familiar two-steps or shuffle steps danced to swing rhythm.

GROUP DANCES

The spirited group dances of yore included grand marches, fandangos and serpentines, quadrilles, lancers (lanciers), cotillions, square dances, germans, reels, longways dances, and mixers, such as the Paul Jones.

Grand March. There were many variations, ranging from a simple promenade of couples down the center of the hall— either in slow- or fast-marching cadence—to a brisk two-step or waltz rhythm to many-faceted figures copied after the lead couple's actions in "follow the leader" style. Some of the figures, each beginning with the promenade, are as follows.

In one form of the serpentine, when the lead couple, trailed by the other dancers, reached the head of the hall, they would turn and double back alongside the column behind them. At the foot of the hall, they would again double back, and so on until the dancers or musicians were exhausted.

For another figure, when the lead couple reached the head of the hall, they would face each other and make an arch by joining both hands in "London Bridge" fashion. They would whisk the arch back over the heads of all the other cou-

ples, who danced under it. Each couple in turn would make an arch and follow them. When the lead couple reached the foot of the line, they would turn and duck under the line of arched hands while returning to the head of the hall, with each of the other couples again following in turn, until all were back in the original column formation.

The "arch and under," or "duck and dive," was also popular. In it the lead couple turned to face the couple behind them and made an arch with only their inside hands joined. This was the signal for all of the couples to join inside hands. The first couple arched over the second couple in line, ducked under an arch made by the third couple, and continued down the line "ducking" and "diving," with each couple following in turn. Bumped heads and great hilarity resulted if a couple ducked when they were supposed to dive.

To form into four-couple groups for any of the quad-formation dances, as the column reached the head of the hall alternate couples turned right and left away from each other and formed two columns. Each column turned back toward the foot at the wall, turned again at the corner, and returned to the starting places at the foot of the hall. When opposite couples met, they linked arms and went down the center in lines of four. They repeated the action by alternating lines of four going right and left. When the lines of four met at the foot of the hall, they went down the center in lines of eight. When the lead line reached the head of the hall, it marked time until all in the group had formed behind it in lines of eight. At that point, either the caller shouted, "Make your lines into squares," or they did another type of serpentine.

For one version of the serpentine, people in each line joined hands and the man at the left end of the front line became the leader. He would turn back and lead his line back and forth through the lines behind him. As they passed, the person at the left end of his line joined hands with the person at the end of the passing line. When the leader had cleared the last line, he pulled the entire line into a large circle facing in. At this point, he could either double back in front of his partner and lead the line "in and out the window" under selected joined hands along the line or "wind 'em up like a ball of twine." To "wind 'em up," he would wind the line into a tight spiral with himself at the center, then unwind it by doubling back along the line as if following a maze.

Single-Line Dances. Couple dances that have been choreographed into spoke-line formation are the schottische, Cotton-eyed Joe, Put Your Little Foot, and the waltz. Ten Pretty Girls is an example of the line schottische.

Four Corners is a rock music, no-hold, drill-line dance that crossed over into the Texas country-dance category in the 1980s. It is performed by dancers staying more or less in one spot and keeping watch to hold the line formation.

One of the earliest no-hold line dances was the Hully Gully, choreographed by a ballroom dance teacher in Dallas. It featured, as does Four Corners, a turning step whereby all dancers form new grid-type lines facing a new direction.

The Freeze is an easy, no-hold, drill-line dance that is quite popular with rock music fans when Texas country musicians play an occasional driving rock-rhythm number. The background is similar to that of the Four Corners.

Quadrille. "Quadrille" was the general term used for the many different formal cotillion and lancers dances. On occasion a dance would be listed simply as a quadrille or a lancers quadrille. Sometimes these names were used interchangeably. Each quadrille had numerous figures. Many of the dances were quite complicated, as the dancing masters vied

with each other in introducing "new" ones. Dancers had to memorize these intricate maneuvers, since the only prompting came with the announcement of the name of the dance. It was imperative also for the social-minded pioneers to learn the styling and to know how to do the different dance steps required during a five- or six-figure cotillion or lancers. The dance steps included the polka, waltz, mazurka, redowa (two-step), and minuet.

Cleveland wrote, "The Lancers quadrille has, of late, superseded the English (or plain) quadrille . . . not many years since, the standard 'square' dance." He then described the following five-figure quadrilles: Prince Imperial Quadrille, to be danced partly in 2/4 and partly in 6/8 time; Les Variétés Parisiennes, first figure, L'Invitation (waltz), second figure, L'Etoile (polka), third figure, Le Prisonnier (waltz), fourth figure, L'Alternate (mazurka or polka redowa), fifth figure, La Rosace (waltz); Waltz Lancers; Waltz Quadrille; and Menuet Quadrille. `

Of Les Variétés Parisiennes, Cleveland wrote, "I consider it the most graceful of all the 'square' dances; the changes from the quadrille movements in 'six-eight' and 'two-four' time to the evolutions of waltz, polka, and polka redowa (or mazurka), lending to it a peculiarly pleasing effect, not only to the dancers themselves, but, when well executed to spectators as well. It is in this dance particularly that knowledge of the time as well as the steps of the round dances is required."

Instructions for part of the second figure read as follows:

Polka movement, "two-four" time. All polka to the right thus: First couple to third couple's place; third couple to second couple's place; second couple to fourth couple's place; fourth couple to first couple's place

. . . . 2 [measures]

All balance, one bar toward the centre
   and the other outward 2
To the right again 2
Balance. 2
To the right again 2
Balance. 2

In the third figure, part of the instructions are as follows:

Waltz movement, "three-four" time.
All turn to the centre (the ladies going
   forward and the gentlemen backward) and form a square, facing outward . . . . 4 [measures]
Turn to places (in waltz positions) . . 4
To the centre again 4
To places 4
Repeat three times; second, third, and
   fourth gentlemen leading, each in
   turn, and always taking the lady on
   the left first, then continue taking
   them from the left until the four
   ladies are forward in circle.

Square Dance. Quadrilles, cotillions, lancers, and square dances are all names for dances performed in the quad- or four-couple square formation, with one couple facing in from each side of the square. The first three were forerunners of the square dance. Pioneer settlers danced infrequently and had difficulty remembering the complicated movements of the formal cotillions, quadrilles, and lancers, so dance leaders and managers, and sometimes the fiddler, began to prompt the dancers with directions as the music was played. This marked the beginnings of square dance calling as we know it today. Eventually, the caller added rhyming patter and singing chants to fill in between the instruction words: "Swing your partner and promenade all; promenade your pretty girl around the hall."

   Square dancing was different—and easier. They jigged, "they shuffled, they wired and they stomped" while the caller improvised the figures and called out directions for simpler figures as the music

was playing. In 1891 a dancing master wrote that "the bane of dancing is the caller." He declared that "persons dancing a quadrille know not what absurd, improper, impolite figures they may be called upon to dance next." Some of the early square dances popular in Texas were called Dip and Dive, Arkansas Traveler, Cage the Bird, and Texas Star.

   Texas Star Call
Ladies to the center, back to the bar,
Gents to the center, make a right hand
   star,
Right hand across, how do you do?
Left hand back, and how are you?
Meet your partner, pass her by,
Pick up the next girl on the fly,
Gents back out, ladies go in,
Make that Texas star again.
Ladies back out, gents go in,
Make that Texas star again.
Break and swing that pretty little thing,
Promenade your new girl around the
   ring.

The men would take new partners with them to their original places and repeat the movements three more times to get their partners back.

German. Cleveland described twenty-nine of the more than one hundred figures in the german: "I have chosen those I consider appropriate for ballrooms and large private parties." Others, he explained, "are adaptable only to the performance of a limited company of intimate acquaintances." Many prizes and favors were accorded for the best performances.

   In regard to favors, he wrote,

The German [the dance] among the ultra fashionable people of our larger cities at one time exercised an objectionable influence on young people, from the extravagance of rivalry in the costliness of the "favors" presented during the performance of certain figures. Diamond rings and studs; fans of ivory and ostrich plumes, inlaid with gold and set with jewels; lace handkerchiefs, opera-chains, toilet-slippers, smoking-caps, and an infinity of other costly trifles,—were offered and accepted between ladies and gentlemen, who in many cases had no other excuses for the extravagance than those of purse pride and personal vanity. . . . It is hoped that the good taste of my pupils will always reject . . . ostentatious vulgarity.

For the german, any number of couples seated themselves in a circle or semicircle, facing in and with ladies to the right of their partners. From his position at the left of a twelve- to fifteen-couple semicircle, or seated in the center facing a larger group, "the conductor and his partner begins the series of figures by waltzing once around the room with his partner; and then designates by signs or verbal instruction such couples as he requires for the execution of particular figures." The signals he used were one clap—form circle; two claps—return to seats; three claps—music cease; four claps—music change (from waltz to polka, polka redowa, or galop).

Instructions for figure 1, La Course, were as follows: "Conductor selects two ladies. His partner selects two gentlemen. Form two lines of threes. Forward and back (eight bars); forward again (four bars), and each lady take opposite gentleman; each gentleman take opposite lady, and turn in place (four bars); all waltz to seats (sixteen bars). N.B.—After placing ladies in their seats, gentlemen will immediately return to their own. (The figures repeated by the next couples in rotation.)"

Figure 16, Les Bouquets, was danced thus: "As many small bouquets as there are dancers in the cotillon. Conductor and his lady each choose a bouquet; and, after waltzing once around, the lady presents hers to another gentleman, and the conductor his to another lady. Re-

peated until all have been presented with bouquets."

Figure 26 was called Les Zigzags: "Any number of couples begin. Place themselves behind each other, with three feet of space between each couple; all facing one way, and keeping close to partners. The first couple sets out and waltzes 'zigzag' through this column, followed by each couple in turn until all are waltzing, then return to seats."

Reel. The most popular and enduring of many reels enjoyed by Texans is the Virginia Reel, derived from the English longways dance, the Sir Roger de Coverly. It was also a favorite of President George Washington. The reel, or longways formation, is made up of a line of men facing a line of women, with partners standing opposite each other. Usually there are five or six couples to a set and the figures are prompted, rather than called as in a square dance.

On being prompted to "salute your partners," those in the lines dance forward and bow to partners, then dance back to place. "Turn partner left" directs partners to dance forward, hook left arms, swing each other all the way around, then return to place. "Head couple reel the line" directs them to right-arm swing each other, alternately with left-arm swings of each of the other couples in turn, going down the line. Each swings the opposite sex. "March to the foot and arch" calls for all to face toward the head of the hall and for partners to separate, turn back, and march along the line to the foot. There they meet each other and make an arch for those following them to pass through. Thus the head couple becomes the foot couple and the second couple becomes the head couple.

SOLO DANCES

Early solo dancing was composed mostly of extemporaneous jigging done by men. The term "jigging" referred to fancy footwork that included clogging, shuffling, leaping, and heel clicking borrowed from Irish jigs, other European dances, and the black influence.

The rapid clatter and thump of lively jigging "making the splinters fly" was often heard at frontier parties, either as side entertainment at the dance parties or in contests. One step, called "cutting the pigeon wing," was done by clapping the feet together while leaping in the air. In a two-person variation, the dancers hooked one or the other of their ankles and, while steadying each other with a handclasp, hopped around each other on the other foot. A "buck-and-wing" was a solo tap dance with sharp accents, springs, leg flings, and heel clicks. There are accounts also of an exuberant square dancer who "wired" and "knocked the back step" while waiting his turn to do the figure. I failed to find a description of these steps, however.

In some places where there were no women, the lonely men had stag parties. In *The Evolution of a State*, Noah Smithwick describes a stag dance held around 1829 in San Felipe, where "some sang, some told stories and some danced." And, "I being the most nimble-footed man in the place, usually paid my dues in jigs and hornpipes, Willie patting [clapping] juba [a complex series of handclapping and knee slapping, of black origin] for me. Many a night was I dragged out of bed after a hard day's work in the shop to help out with an impromptu 'jag.'"

Later, as the big ranches developed, the cowboys would gather around the campfire in the evening after the work was done to watch a spirited dancer do a fancy clog dance while the fiddler sawed out a rousing reel or hoedown.

MIXER DANCES

In pioneer days, when there were more men than women, mixer dances were very popular. On signal, romantically inclined extra men standing inside a circle of dancers were permitted to rush forward and claim another's partner during a certain segment of a dance.

Mixers have long been incorporated into old-time structured dances done in various formations, such as those used in longways, rounds, circles, and squares. Various devices have been used to instigate a change of partner: voice commands to promenading couples for the men to "roll back and take a new partner"; the Tucker Waltz, which alternates three-count music with four-count, allowing extra men to grab a partner at the time of the change; or blowing a whistle or ringing a bell to signal a change.

Mixers are popular these days at some private social dances but are not usually promoted at public dances. They are used as "ice breakers" to liven the occasion by getting people to dance together without the formalities of introductions or individual invitations. Mixers are gestures of friendliness used to help people get acquainted quickly while dancing for a short time with several different partners during one number.

Paul Jones. One of the early versions of the old-time Paul Jones dance was called Circle Two-step. It was danced as a circle dance following square dance–type calls, alternating with couple two-step dancing. Couples formed a circle and followed such calls as "circle left," "circle right," "grand right and left"; then "form a double circle, ladies on the inside facing out, gents on the outside facing in"; followed by "join hands and everybody circle, left [or right]." The circles of people with joined hands thus went in opposite directions. On the call, "everybody dance," or "everybody two-step," or simply "Paul Jones," each man danced the two-step with the woman facing him. Those unable to find a partner at once went to the center of the hall to pair up. Couples intermingled with other dancers on the floor until the call sounded to "form a grand circle with your lady on your right," to begin again.

3

Music and Musicians

The wail and sigh of the fiddle were the musical sounds that started toes to tapping at most early Texas dances, although in some instances pianos and other instruments had been laboriously hauled in by freight wagons. Army regiments had brass bands that played for civilian as well as military dances, and an occasional musician "blew up a dance tune" on a French harp. Along the musical instrument frontier in Stephen F. Austin's colony were "German jews-harps," a piano or two, and several guitars, flutes, and fiddles. By 1846 nearly every river valley had at least one piano and other instruments, and instances were not unknown in which the mahogany legs of pianos rested on the dirt floors of log cabins. But fiddles (not violins) were usually the first musical instruments brought into new settlements.

Yet music for dances was not available everywhere, so when an itinerant stranger with a fiddle hung in a flour sack from his saddle rode into an isolated community that had no musician, there was great rejoicing. A dance with "everyone invited" was usually arranged at once, even if it was a week day. Although fiddlers were often considered ne'er-do-wells, as reflected in such expressions as "lazy enough to be a good fiddler," at dances they were treated with great respect by folks eager to "swing your pardner," or "gallop around in a promenade."

If more than one fiddler was available, they took turns sawing out the reels and quadrilles, and in the nineteenth and early twentieth centuries, black fiddlers were quite common in Texas. They added an enriching syncopation to the old tunes brought from the British Isles and other European countries by immigrants. The terms "hoedown" and "breakdown," applied to a fast, rollicking way of playing an accompaniment to a lively, shuffling-type of dancing, are probably also of black origin. A jiglike dance of black origin (the juba) was accompanied by complex rhythmic hand clapping and slapping of the knees and thighs. A good juba clapper was in great demand for jigging, even when other music was available.

Some musicians with deft bow arms played for the pure pleasure of it, without pay. For others, the hat might be passed among the merry dancers at a public dance, and each man was expected to contribute either two bits or four bits. At other dances held in homes, each man paid from five cents to twenty-five cents for each time he got to dance. Since there were always many more men than women, and limited space usually allowed for only one or two squares (four couples to each square) to dance at once, there was a manager who kept a list, and the men took turns dancing. Sometimes an eager swain would buy another man's place in order to do a lively schottische with a particularly attractive partner. Depending on how many dancers were present, the fiddler or fiddlers might earn from twenty-five cents to thirty dollars a night. Musicians usually received extra pay for playing after midnight. One cowhand, who earned thirty dollars as a fiddler in addition to his salary during Christmas week in 1860, said later, "It was almost enough to retire on."

Sometimes, when music was unavailable or inadequate, the lonely settlers, desperate for social pleasures to lighten the hardships of pioneer life, would devise substitutes to provide rhythm for dancing. One such substitute was a clevis and a pin. The clevis is a U-shaped metal fastening device with the ends pierced for a bolt or pin. It was used to attach parts of a wagon to each other. The clevis made a loud ringing noise when the pin was struck against it and was used much as triangles are today to beat out time. At an 1833 dance in Harrisburg, music was provided by three black fiddlers playing in turn, accompanied by "an iron pin and clevis." In one instance when the fiddler failed to show, an old slave was called in to beat out time on a clevis, "while another Negro scraped on a cotton hoe with a case knife." W. R. Hogan, in *The Texas Republic*, recalls that once when a "fiddler got drunk . . . a captain, who couldn't play, picked up the fiddle and sawed on the strings . . . patted his foot . . . and called." The eager dancers continued.

In *Oldtimers of Southwest Texas*, Florence Fenley quotes Mrs. Verna Armstrong, an early resident in the Uvalde area, who describes another substitute for a musical instrument: "Whenever something went wrong with the fiddle, Ike O'Bryant would make the music with a leaf. You wouldn't think you could make dance music with a peach leaf, but he would put it in his lips and blow it and we would dance like it was the best music in the world." In Comfort, the music sometimes consisted of blowing on a comb through a thin piece of paper, the ringing of bells, or rhythmical tapping against drinking glasses for a musical sound.

A small grand piano of mahogany and rosewood, brought by a doctor in 1856, took three months to travel from Tennessee to Louisiana by water, then to Fort Worth by oxcart. About the same time, a couple in West Texas had a small folding organ freighted to the Bar CC Ranch from Dodge City. These homes were centers of social life and dancing.

On special occasions, musicians were brought in from long distances. For the

1885 Cowboy's Christmas Ball at Anson, a bass viol was brought from Abilene, 30 miles away, to round out "a fiddle, tambourine and banjo" band. The Matador Ranch got an orchestra from Childress, 65 miles away, for its 1895 Valentine dance, and Wichita Falls celebrated the first anniversary of the arrival of the railroad by importing two fiddlers and a caller from Dallas, 130 miles away. For a special dance held in the schoolhouse near Dalhart in the late 1800s, musicians from Colorado were paid eighty-five dollars, and there was a *woman* caller. Bands, either from Mexican settlements near the posts or regimental bands from the troops, were usually available for military dances. Mexican fandangos relied on fiddles and guitars.

In the larger towns, especially Austin, there were more choices. At a ball in Austin in 1850, "General Harney's fine band . . . discoursed most eloquent music." In 1874 at a "Social Hop . . . the brass band from the garrison was stationed on the balcony," and "the social opened with a grand march from the excellent string band." At the 1881 Final Ball for the University of Texas, held in the Driskill Hotel for six hundred young people, "the Twenty-third infantry band discoursed sweet music."

The people of Texas expected governors to begin their terms with two big social events—an inaugural ball and a levee for the legislature. At the inaugural ball for Governor Oran M. Roberts in 1879, everyone paid five dollars to attend the dance, with music provided by a string band that "played mostly waltzes and Virginia reels."

In connection with the 1888 dedication of the Texas state capitol, elegant balls were held in the library, the House of Representatives, and the Senate chamber. "The music was furnished by the famous Gilmore band, the Mexican National band, the U.S. 16th Infantry band, and four other bands." At the second an-

nual encampment of the Texas Volunteer
Guard of 1892, there was a "massed
Military Band of 500 pieces." In Austin
in 1893, the steamboat *Dixie* towed a
launch behind it carrying a Mexican
band to play for dancing, and for the University Final Ball in 1895, the Fifth Cavalry band played.

The Hoggs were a zestful, fun-loving
family, and Sallie, the governor's wife,
was an accomplished pianist. Frequent
informal parties in 1895 included the
children and their friends, who square
danced and did Virginia reels, schottisches, and polkas in the mansion.
Around 1900, Austin was blessed with
Professor William Besserer and his eight-
piece string band.

Many of the dances held in the capital
were subscription dances, and gentlemen
were "requested to make early applica-
tion" for tickets to complimentary balls.
At an Austin fund-raising ball in 1875,
"about $100 was raised toward furnish-
ing the Oddfellows new hall." In February 1896, a "grand charity ball" given at
the Driskill Hotel to benefit the Eye, Ear
and Throat Hospital preceded the Lenten
"breathing spell" in the social season.

4

Homespuns and Satins, Buckskins and Boughten Suits

Clothing worn to dances held in the raw wilderness of early Texas was as widely varied in style, material, and tailoring as were the personalities of the polyglot of people who chose to cast their lot on the frontier. The elite arrived with trunks packed with the latest fashions from Europe or New York; others, of more humble circumstances, or by choice, made do with homemade frontier garb. Nevertheless, they danced —at every opportunity—even to the point of sharing clothing if need be.

Noah Smithwick, who came to Texas in 1827, tells in *The Evolution of a State* of a notable wedding dance given by socially prominent families from Austin's colony. The rough floor was made of puncheons (split logs). Dancing was vigorous in those days, with loud stamping and jigging calling for sturdy footgear. Some of the men attending had only soft moccasins, so their more fortunate friends generously let them take a turn at wearing their shoes so they could "stomp the splinters off 'til dawn." Of a San Antonio ball in the 1840s, Mary Maverick recorded in her *Memoirs* that three men "had but one dress coat between them," so they took turns wearing it. To the same dance, Gen. Mirabeau B. Lamar wore wide white pants, and one woman wore "a maroon cashmere with black plumes in her hair."

The clothing was not always terribly comfortable for exuberant dancing. Mary Maverick recalls that one lady wearing a tight corset at a dance was "several times compelled to escape to her bedroom" and "catch her breath."

Another wedding ball described by Smithwick was held in Bastrop, at a home with "a good plank floor." The bridegroom, a merchant, wore "store clothes," but there were many homespuns "and the old reliable buckskin was also in evidence." The ladies wore silks in varied styles, "depending on the period when the wearer migrated thither." Smithwick himself "was resplendent in a brand new buckskin suit, consisting of hunting shirt, pantaloons and moccasins, all elaborately fringed."

John R. Craddock, in *The Cowboy Dance*, describes a square dance caller as someone "forward and loud-mouthed" wearing fancy boots and lock-roweled spurs with rattlesnake skin covering his belt, buckled on the side instead of in the center. A "fancy patterned and flaming colored shirt—stamped leather collar with a gaudy tie with a small circle from a cow's horn instead of a knot. A pair of new buckskin gloves hung from the pocket of his 'peg-topped' trousers and a Bull Durham tag hung from a sack in his shirt pocket."

Frank Gray, in *Pioneering in Southwest Texas*, describes a dance in what is now Edwards County: "The girls who came on horseback rode sidesaddles. They wore becoming hats, long sleeves, long skirts, high collars, high topped low heel shoes, obscured from view by their long attractive black riding habits that reached to their horses' knees. Being December, they wore heavy clothing . . . and to be fashionable, they wore bustles and corsets." One girl wore a striking wrap made from the spotted fur of an ocelot killed by her father. "Their long hair was done up neatly around their heads. . . . The young men wore their best clothes, never appeared in the ballroom without their coats and never danced with their hats on or their pants in their boots."

For dances on the XIT Ranch, ranchers short of cash would borrow clothing from a store, and cowboys in boots left

Early-day square dancing; due to a shortage of women, some men wore aprons and took their place. Courtesy the *Cattleman* magazine.

off their spurs and wore the trousers outside instead of tucked in, "in deference to the women." Many "wore dancing shoes." Most of the women wore their hair in the latest pompadour and curled their own hair by heating the curling irons over "a coaloil lamp." Dresses almost touched the floor and "were tight as beeswax," reported Mrs. C. R. Duke of the XIT. Lipstick, rouge, and permanents were unknown.

One dress worn to dances in the tiny Texas Panhandle town of Mobeetie in the 1880s had a "bottle-green basque brocaded velvet top with a white, ruffled organdy skirt." Another was of worsted cloth with a flounce below the knee. The flounce had a heading lined with black satin and gathered at intervals to form diamond shapes. In West Texas, for Saturday night dances held every two weeks at the ranches, a cowboy knocked

off as soon after noon as possible to get ready. He "borrowed a washtub from headquarters, heated buckets of water on the bunkhouse box heater, then bathed in gyp [gypsum] water with laundry soap, and shaved with a straight razor." From an old suitcase under the bed, "he took out his Sunday suit, clean but wrinkled shirt, detached collar and ready-tied cravat with an imitation pearl in the center." He also dragged out low-quarter shoes "to be tied onto his saddle, or rolled up in his slicker, and put on when he reached the dance." No self-respecting cowboy would ride a horse without boots.

In the Nueces River canyon in the 1800s, the girls in one family had two dresses each, one calico dress for school and one nice dress for special occasions, such as dances or church. Special dresses were made of satin, which cost fifteen cents a yard (cotton was five cents). They went barefooted at home until they were grown.

One woman declared she'd never dance on a rough puncheon floor again, because "she wore out a two-dollar pair of slippers at the last dance." One man, "diked out fit to kill in my ruffled-bosomed shirt, standing collar and white necktie," was ostracized by the girls because they didn't like his attire.

At Uvalde dances the boys and men wore "three button cutaway sacks and loud stiff-bosomed shirts with the coat lapels rolled back to show them off." Some of the shirts "even had pansies on 'em" and the suits were usually black or navy blue. One lady reported in Florence Fenley's *Oldtimers of Southwest Texas* that "our ball dresses didn't cost much and may not sound like they were very pretty when I tell you they were made of cheese cloth, but they were lovely. You would see blue, pink, cream, red, pale green and maybe other colors, and they were made long; almost reached the floor." Sometimes the girls would make an apron and tie of the same material. At the dance, the ties were put in a grab bag and the men drew for partners.

In more-populated areas with a higher level of sophistication and greater affluence, costumes worn to formal balls were more stylish and elegant. The *Houston Chronicle* carried an account written by Mrs. A. B. Looscan from her mother's notes of an 1837 San Jacinto ball. It was the first social function held in the nine-month-old town of Houston after it became the capital of the new Texas Republic in 1837.

Many came from as far as sixty miles away and some came up the bayou in rowboats, accompanied by servants who had charge of their elegant costumes. Some of those attending changed into party clothes at the home of General Baker, where the dirt floor of the large room was covered by a carpet. General Houston wore a ruffled shirt, scarlet

cashmere waistcoat, and black silk-velvet suit corded with gold. His short boots with folded-down red tops were set off by silver spurs. The women's low-cut, short-sleeved dresses included one of white satin with black lace overdress. At the hall, "the ladies laid aside their wraps and changed from black shoes to white satin slippers."

About another San Jacinto ball in 1838, Mrs. Mary Austin Holley, Stephen F. Austin's cousin, wrote in a letter, "Everything available for dresses in Texas had been bought up. . . . Confectionery and ornaments . . . are to be brought by Columbia [steamboat] from New Orleans." She noted that the men dressed "remarkably well" in clothes of the newest fashion from New York.

Government social functions in the state capital, after it was moved to Austin in 1840, involved many dances with varying degrees of elegance reflecting the personalities involved. Governor Roberts and his wife, Frances, had a simple and unpretentious lifestyle during his term (1879 to 1883). For all state occasions, she wore "a good, plain black silk gown." Anna Maria Ireland did not attend the ball for her husband's inauguration in 1883 because she did not believe in dancing.

Costumes for other grand balls were flamboyantly elegant. From the *Austin Statesman* we learn that the "magnificent" ball in 1888, held in three rooms of the capitol to celebrate the new building's dedication, was attended by "throngs" from high-society circles and distinguished guests from Mexico and England. Handsome cadets wore white uniforms to the dance. Lizzie Ross, the governor's matronly wife, "was impressive in a gown of black lace over moire antique silk with jet trimmings and ruby accessories." Miss Florine Ross, "the governor's beautiful and accomplished daughter, looked charming in an exquisite train dress of pale pink and blue moire silk and pink tulle draped with lilies of the valley." Others at the affair wore "cream white, with draperies of point lace, embroidered in silk and chenille flowers tipped with rhinestones," "pink marveleaux silk handsomely trimmed with pink pearl passementerie," "an imported costume of heliotrope embroidered bolting cloth, faille silk court train [and] ruby velvet, pink moire front, court train." One lady was "magnificent in primrose yellow faille silk, embossed velvet and point lace," and many wore diamonds. Most of the dresses were décolleté and sleeveless.

A newspaper reported that at a lavish dinner and ball for Governor Hogg's inaugural in 1891 those attending "pressed their way through embankments of silks, satins, decollete gowns and broad white shirt fronts." In 1899 Fannie Sayers, the governor's wife, was elegant at a ball in a gown of white Batenburg lace with simple pearl accessories.

Alice Colquitt liked white clothing. She chose a white lace dress with pearls and white satin shoes with beads and carried a white lace fan to her husband's inaugural ball in 1911. In 1915, newly elected Governor Ferguson made a striking figure in a cutaway coat at inaugural balls held in three locations: the Senate chamber, the Austin Hotel, and the Driskill Hotel. His wife, Miriam, was the belle of the balls in a handsome gown of heavily beaded, flesh-pink chiffon.

At military balls, the men turned out smartly in full-dress uniforms. There were many masquerade balls, and costumes worn included a seventeenth-century character, Old Bruin, a Black Knight, and Undine in ferns, mosses, and seashells. At a military "masque ball" held in Brackettville, an officer showed up encased in a mattress.

One couple attending a fancy-dress costume ball at Fort Concho in 1876 represented the queen of hearts and jack of clubs by sewing playing cards onto their clothing. There was also a Swiss peasant costume, a novice taking the veil, and a clown in a yellow suit.

5

Dancing Was Lively despite Obstacles

Despite seemingly insurmountable physical, and sometimes moral, obstacles, Texas pioneers danced at every opportunity—and the dancing was lively! Everybody seized on any excuse to have a dance: a wedding, house-raising, christening, roundup, holiday, inaugural, birthday, whim, or even a funeral. Romance and dance marked time with the galloping of horses and the roar of rifle fire.

Physical Obstacles

They were a social people who disregarded hardships and devised ingenious "make-dos" for the dance to go on. They used garlands of fresh greenery to camouflage grim settings, cooked mounds of food to share at festivities, and braved the threat of unfriendly Indians, mud, fire, greedy neighbors, and pranks. They overcame a lack of facilities and women partners, a plentiful supply of vicious weather, grueling travel for long distances, and even duels. Many accounts of those challenging days illustrate methods of injecting gaiety into the grim realities of their lives.

Texas was called a bachelor republic because "women were scarce in this man's world, and single women of courting size almost nonexistent." The man who wrote this said of one dance that the men had been "so crazy" after the women, he had contented himself with partnering an eleven-year-old girl. Men sometimes even resorted to dancing with each other to satisfy their need for social entertainment. At a dance for the cowhands only on the Slaughter Ranch, there were no women at all to dance with. The man who took the part of the "lady fair" or was "heifer branded" wore either a handkerchief tied around his arm or a ruffled skirt, probably borrowed from the foreman's wife, tucked into the front of his belt.

One early settler reported that "the gentle sex were few in number at the dance, only three young married women. Two men had to dance together to make up a set." At another dance, "due to the scarcity of young women, a number of the younger bachelors who were either smooth shaven or wore polished shoes were designated as ladies."

Out in ranch country, where the men stayed at distant cow camps for long periods of time, the women would visit them on holidays and weekends. They'd share a meal from the chuckwagon, then the musicians would tune up fiddles and guitars, someone would spread a wagon sheet over the prairie dog holes, grass burrs, and dusty ground, and the dance would be on—under a blazing midday sun.

A description of dances held at Fort Clark explained that they were held anywhere there was space—in a mess hall, an empty hospital ward, or in the schoolhouse chapel. The band set up in the middle of the hall and separated the officers at one end from the enlisted men at the other. Soldiers danced with laundresses, servants, women from the vicinity, and each other. Officers danced with wives, daughters, sweethearts, and "proper" women from the vicinity.

At times the travel related to the dance was a major part of the activity. The hardy dancers jolted in wagons and hacks or on horseback for great distances or slogged "through horrible roads of mud and slush" to get to the socials. Dances lasted all night because nighttime travel was hazardous owing to the need for light on rough trails and roads and the danger from Indians or wild animals.

An old-time range "stag" dance; cowboys two-stepped and waltzed with each other at woman-less dances; a handkerchief tied around one arm designated the partner who was "heifer branded." Courtesy the *Cattleman* magazine.

Dancing on a wagon sheet, early 1900s, at the Swenson SMS Ranch near Stamford, Texas; on weekends and holidays the cowpunchers' families and friends visited at the chuckwagon site to eat and frolic. Courtesy Jenkins Publishing Company, Austin, Texas.

Mary Austin Holley wrote of "a great ball at Velasco" in 1837. "It rains today, however we are going . . . in a small covered wagon (without spring seats). . . . The steamboat . . . on the Brazos will fetch and carry the people." A Mrs. Gerlach told of going to dances at the Sutherland Hotel in Canadian. They had to cross the Canadian River in a wagon at flood time to reach the dance.

"Mud, Mud, Mud" was the headline in an Austin newspaper in 1887. The article declared that it was a disgrace to a town of five thousand persons that a few hours' rain turned the streets of the capital "into a veritable hog-wallow," resulting in wading through "six inches of mud and slop" to cross the street. According to a newspaper editorial in November 1893, it was still a problem. "Not since Austin was a frontier town, raided by Indians, have the streets been in as bad condition as now," they wrote. This was at a time when Austin was a veritable beehive of social activity, with dances practically every evening during "the season"—September to June. Of one elaborate "masque ball" held at the capitol in Austin on a rainy night, it was reported that, although they had spent much effort in preparing "ingenious" costumes, many stayed home because the muddy streets were impassable. Nevertheless, those who braved the elements danced "with high spirits."

Cowboys "spruced up and hired a buggy from a livery stable at the nearest town" if they could. "One man's girl lived 12 miles from the ranch where he worked. He rode 24 miles to ask her. Then he rode sixteen miles to town and 16 miles back to get the buggy, then drove 12 miles to the girl's home, and to the dance covering eight miles. Afterward he drove eight miles back to the girl's house, 12 miles to the ranch, and made the 32 mile round trip to return the buggy. In all 128 miles in order to take his best girl to the dance." Another

young man had to "shoe both horses all around" for a day's ride with his sister to a dance, "over a rough, rocky country."

Lew Bradley convinced Emmet Price to "beat those other cowboys' time with the Cox sisters" by hiring a hack to take them to the dance celebrating the new courthouse opening at Amarillo in 1889. The hack was in Amarillo and the girls lived forty-five miles away in Tascosa. Two days before the dance, the men made the all-day ride into Amarillo on their cow ponies to get the hack. The next day was spent going to the girls' house. Sunrise on the third day saw the two couples "wrapped in suggans [coarse blankets]" on their way to Amarillo. The trip was made enjoyable by a picnic lunch of fried antelope steak, wild plum pie, sourdough biscuit and bean sandwiches, and thick chunks of gold cake. They sang on their way to the good time ahead.

The new Amarillo Hotel was crowded when they arrived, so the girls were assigned makeshift beds with two other women on the floor of the hotel parlor. After the opening grand march, the dancing started with a square dance called in cowboy vernacular:

Heifers in the middle, strays outside,
Swing your partners, swing 'em wide.

Following a midnight feast and dancing until four in the morning, the men dropped by the saloon next door before bedding down on the suggans under the hack in the livery stable. In the hotel parlor, the four girls put on night clothes, then discovered that the kerosene lamp hanging in a gilt-and-red-glass chandelier could not be pulled down and they could not blow out the light. Even on a chair they couldn't reach it, nor did fanning their petticoats put out the light, so they decided to sleep with it on.

While turning over, one of the girls flipped a blanket against a closely drawn shade, causing it to roll up to the top. The startled girls discovered that the window was directly opposite the crowded saloon's window, from which came a loud guffaw. Undaunted, the girls held the counterpane in front of them, went to the window and pulled the shade down, and then, after a giggle-fest, slept until dawn.

On the fourth day the couples returned home, on the fifth the cowboys returned the hack, and on the sixth they rode their cow ponies back to the ranch. Six days of riding had been spent to enjoy seven hours of dancing pleasure.

On Christmas Day in 1898, when Bob Duke was "baching" at Alamocitas line camp on the XIT Ranch, he rode twenty-five miles to call for a dance in the courthouse at Tascosa. He was eager to use new calls from Kansas, which he had already tried out on some visiting cowboys with a black cowboy doing the fiddling. His trusty horse, Monkeyface, carried him across the rock-bottomed Canadian River in three feet of water lined with ice along the banks. The dance was especially merry because "a fellow brought in some girls from the north flats, and they sure could dance."

When his numbered turn to dance came up, he invited Miss McKay to be his partner for the next set. He called "three by nine in a pokey-oh" to the music of "Ta-rah-rah, Boom de-ay" while dancing enthusiastically at the same time. About ten o'clock a norther blew in and by two it was "near zero," but the dance was a huge success.

On the way home the next morning, Duke accompanied the carriage with the girls to the fork of the road, lingered to watch as they turned off, then started his lonely way home. They had begged him to stop nearby at a hotel, but he insisted on going home. Creeks he crossed were frozen solid enough for Monkeyface to walk on, but the horse broke through the ice on the river, dumping Bob in the freezing water. His clothing froze so stiff he couldn't walk, but he was able to pull

himself up into the saddle and make it back to camp.

Bob unsaddled Monkeyface and fed him in the barn, then built a roaring fire in the fireplace, went to bed, and piled blankets over his shivering body. Chills and chest pains plagued him for several days and he was sure he looked death in the face. He vowed that if God let him live he would not be so foolhardy again. He reflected that dancing was not wrong, but riding fifty miles in freezing weather to do it was going to an extreme. At last his fever subsided and the sun came out. He continued to call for XIT dances but never danced again.

In 1843 there was a rural wedding and dance near Huntsville. "About midnight the elderly and mothers with babies departed, the road being lighted by Negroes who went ahead with firepans of the type used in deer hunting. But the younger guests danced until dawn."

On the Bar CC Ranch in 1886, when Mrs. Todd joined in efforts to give the cowboys a real Christmas celebration, hard-to-come-by supplies were freighted in by barrels and the barren countryside was scoured for cedar boughs and other appropriate decorations. A boy rode 120 miles to a store and back for candles to decorate the many-tiered cake, each tier baked by a different cowboy. Noah, the black cook, provided six wild turkeys for the feast. Cowboys came from five counties and danced all night with every available girl or woman in the area.

"One year there was a Christmas Eve dance in the courthouse [at Mobeetie], and one every night until sunup through the next week. 'Many's the time I've walked seven or eight miles to a party, danced and sung calls all at the same time all night long, and got home just when the sun was coming up,' recalled Fat Murrell." Often, a dance would turn into a house party lasting several days.

The girls were as eager for the dances as the cowboys. Ina Chillcut of West

Texas recalled that girlfriends of hers from as far away as Trinidad, Colorado, and Clarendon, Texas, would manage to visit her if a dance was in prospect. "We girls would help the boys mow the hay—do anything to get through—have supper, and go to the bunkhouse to dance," she said. "Once we had a dancing master, who also played the violin; he taught us many steps. We not only danced at the ranch, but would hitch a team to the hack and go 31 miles to Clayton, New Mexico to dances. Sometimes we would go to Texline, leave the team, go up on the train, come back, get the team and go back to the ranch."

Although living conditions were crude, the socially inclined outdid themselves when it came to decorating for events. The buildings were unpainted and ugly, there was no running water, outhouses prevailed, and makeshift arrangements were necessary when preparing for a large crowd. The arrangement committees had their work cut out for them, but they met the challenge.

Houston was but nine months old when it became capital of the Republic of Texas in 1837. It was little more than a name, and its two thousand inhabitants lived in tents and temporary structures of clapboards and pine poles on the banks of the bayou. Nevertheless, a large, elegant inaugural ball was arranged for the first president, Gen. Sam Houston. A large unfinished building, twenty-five by seventy-five feet, was hastily made into a dance hall. Pine boughs covered the open rafters, and wooden crosspieces hung from the ceiling served as chandeliers holding sperm oil candles, which dripped on the gorgeous costumes.

An Austin ball honoring Col. William G. Cook in 1841 achieved acclaim for its splendid decorations. The railings, tables, desks, and lobby seats were removed from the Senate chamber at the capitol. Walls were decorated with "festoons, pyramids, wreaths and stars of evergreen

. . . drapery of blue, white and red . . . flags of Texas, the United States and France, and an immense Texian flag formed a panoply on the ceiling." A "stand of muskets, polished to dazzling brightness, with bayonets fixed ranged from one end to the other, leaving only space sufficient at each end for a promenade around the stand. The room was illuminated by two large chandeliers formed by inverted bayonets rising in a conical form . . . suspended from the ceiling."

Dances were held on platforms set up on lawns in the summer, because it was cooler outside. The platforms were also decorated attractively; flags and bunting fluttered in the breeze under soft lighting from Chinese lanterns. One year the Driskill Hotel was decorated with five thousand gardenias, two thousand yards of smilax, and two wagonloads of maidenhair fern for a University of Texas commencement ball. To add cheer and liveliness, "hundreds of young people were liberally splashed with 60 gallons of champagne."

The ability to "make do" and look on the bright side made life bearable for the people whose destinies cast them into the beginning of the saga of the Lone Star State. An account in *Frontier Forts of Texas* quotes memoirs in which the wife of Capt. O. B. Boyd wrote about army life at Fort Clark in the 1870s. Their enthusiasm for dancing was remarkable: "A large ball was given on our arrival, and the different posts at which we had stopped en route—Fort Bliss, Davis, and Stockton—had all honored us in the same way."

They remained at Fort Clark ten days without housing and finally moved into "a very comfortable little house, built of limestone, and charming as to exterior . . . for even in the month of February vines covered the veranda." The family had only one room with a double bed and a lounge for the children at night.

Mrs. Boyd swung a hammock over the bed for a cradle. "No other army post has ever been the scene of so constant a succession of regimental changes." They were near the border where marauding bands of Indians or horse thieves captured herds of cattle from neighboring ranches and slipped over the border with them. This called for large contingents of soldiers for protection:

We were, however, very gay through all our miseries and deprivations; for with seventy-five officers and forty ladies in the garrison many pleasures could be enjoyed. During the first winter we had a series of balls for the exchange of regimental courtesies. Those already stationed at Fort Clark gave a large ball to welcome the newcomers . . . which courtesy was returned by a very grand affair. Then each regiment—six were represented, two of them colored—extended hospitalities on its individual account and each vied with the others in somewhat varying the character of the entertainment.

Following that, the bachelors gave a large german where the favors were superb. Then the ladies united in a New Year's reception, which was said to surpass all the rest. Afterward we had weekly hops, a masquerade and phantom party, at which it was difficult to hide our identity. . . . Probably the officer who entered the room encased in a well-stuffed mattress did so most effectually.

They rejoiced in the opportunity to give balls in honor of the many high-ranking visiting officers or inspectors. Since half of the officers stationed there were in the cavalry, riding and driving parties were also "indulged in daily." "One night I shall never forget. The moon shone her best and brightest on a smooth stretch of canvas, spread so as to form a splendid dancing-floor, and on

trees hung with fairy lanterns, which extending as far as the eye could reach met as background the pretty little stream on whose banks lovers wandered."

Although rumors of war kept increasing, a truce was arranged with Mexico: "Courtesies were exchanged between leading officers in the Mexican and American armies, which we shared in by giving a grand ball to the general and staff of the Mexican army on their visit to our post while negotiating terms of peace. Our third winter at Fort Clark was brilliant socially."

Many other pioneer Texans demonstrated the resilience and adaptability displayed by Mrs. Boyd. Everybody worked for weeks in advance preparing for the dinner, speeches, and dance held on July 4, 1854, in Marble Falls. The mills donated flour to be used in baking; men brought in wagonloads of watermelons, cantaloupes, roasting ears, and vegetables. Others brought venison, wild turkeys, beef, and pork, and there were cakes and pies—wild grape, dewberry, and wild plum. An arbor covered with brush was erected to cover a speakers' stand and seating for the audience, and the ground underneath it was "carpeted with a thick layer of sawdust, which served for a dancing floor."

A unique seat was rigged up for Herman Schimmelpfennig, the fiddler in the village of Comfort: "Dances were staged either in larger rooms or private homes in the winter, whereas the grassy spot under the live oaks . . . (in summer) served as the dance floor. In these trees a saddle was swung over a low-hanging limb; Schimmelpfennig was hoisted into this 'comfortable' seat, and the dance was on." The tree is still referred to as the Schimmelpfennig Eiche.

On New Year's Eve, 1875, Colonel and Mrs. Grierson entertained the post at Fort Concho with an elaborate party. The weather was stormy and rainy, but "the dancing was lively," Mrs. Grierson wrote.

A sophisticated new arrival at the post with her husband gave her impressions of a dance: "I nearly killed myself laughing. It was a regular frontier dance with the most absurd old Negro to call off the most ridiculous quadrilles, and everyone danced in true Negro style."

Regardless of diligent efforts to ensure the comfort and enjoyment of the dancers, mishaps did occur. A report noted that President Anson Jones' wife, Mary, momentarily expecting a child, did not attend his inaugural ball on December 9, 1844, above Hatfield's Saloon: "Thus she missed . . . the highlight of the ball when a very attractive, very popular, rather large young woman began to sink through the floor boards to the saloon below. Sam Houston had had the stairs moved out to stop lawmakers from slipping down to the saloon, and carpenters had failed to nail down the boards that covered the empty stairwell. Fortunately, the lady was pulled to safety by some of the gentlemen present."

In Florence Fenley's *Oldtimers: Their Own Stories*, we learn of a social affair held in an unusual spot near Uvalde in the 1800s:

> We had a real weddin' in camp one night. We knowed for a week or two it was coming off and we made lots of preparations. . . . We had plenty of fine barbecued meat, bread, coffee and drinks and a big bunch from town come out with the girl and brought the squire. We was camped right in the bed of a creek. We had cleaned off a big, flat rock to dance on and we had worked on it two weeks, smoothing it and sanding it and we sure had it nice.

> When the girl got there, they stretched up a canvas on some bushes for her party and she met Huff at the flat rock. The cowboys was all standing 'round in their boots, spurs and leggin's just like they was starting out to work. The folks had brought a fid-

Sunset-to-sunrise, weekend-long dance party, 1897, on the Frying Pan Ranch north of Amarillo; the ladies removed their belts "to give a flowing Grecian robe effect." Courtesy Panhandle-Plains Historical Museum, Canyon, Texas.

dler along and after the ceremony, we started dancing. The bride and groom slipped off and went home about 4 o'clock in the morning. We all went on dancing and had one grand celebration.

Most people were considerate and contributed a fair share toward the festivities, but deadbeats and greedy settlers were not unknown. In 1855 the Masonic hall at Burnet was dedicated with a "grand barbecue and ball." The ample dinner was free to all, but "there were quantities appropriated by the outside element." One fellow was seen "riding off on horseback with a quarter of roasted beef on his shoulder."

At a San Antonio party given by Mary Maverick in the 1840s, "a freezing norther blew in" and they had "the excellent good luck of making some ice cream. . . . Those of the Mexicans present, who had never tasted it . . . all admired and liked it." On the disagreeable side, however, "some natives remained so late in the morning, we had to ask them to go," and "one man . . . carried off a roast chicken . . . another a carving knife. . . . others took off all the cake they could well conceal."

Smithwick reports that

the houses of the early Texans were small but their hearts were large enough to cover all deficiencies. No candidate for hospitality was ever turned away. Free food was a common ingredient of all early day socials and dances. A long table was set up in the yard for weddings, school events and Masonic and holiday dances. These free-for-all dinners were discontinued after a few years; the hungry hordes that swarmed in from all parts of the country, not content with a hearty dinner, filled their pockets, reticules, baskets and handkerchiefs with the dessert provided by the ladies, till they went on a strike against the imposition, and thereafter only those having the password gained admittance.

In *Combats and Conquests of Immortal Heroes*, Charles M. Barnes tells us that fandangos held in early San Antonio, for both the rich and poor, were marred by the ever-present "deadly *duells*." At one time, "they were so commonplace that the incidents of the duello never disturbed the progress of the dance." At a fandango held in a building at Flores and Nueva streets, "a very tall and pretty American met death in the middle of the floor when the dance was at its zenith. The corpse was hastily removed while the dance, but momentarily halted, was resumed before the body was hastily flung on the floor of an adjoining room."

Unfriendly Indians were another ever-present threat on the frontier. While the fiddle "enlivened the atmosphere, and dancers waltzed and knocked the backstep" at a dance in East Texas, a band of Indians stealthily crept to the corral where the horses were penned. By the time they were discovered, most of the horses were disappearing with them into the woods. Fortunately, a few horses were tied to trees and wagons, so the revelers were not left entirely without transportation.

One old-timer told of traveling through the countryside to attend a dance at a ranch. He and his friend, two young ladies, and their two brothers had set out early in the morning. There was no road, and about ten miles along the way, "just after crossing a small stream," they saw a party of "perhaps fifteen Indians who had drawn up and were sitting upon their horses looking at us." The Indians kept their distance but followed them for about an hour, then quickly rode off. "The four men in our party were well armed," he noted, "and but for the presence of the two young ladies we would have attacked the Indians." They continued to the ranch and danced "till nearly dawn."

Mary Maverick of San Antonio tells in her *Memoirs* of another type of altercation with an Indian in 1836. "One day, Old 'Bowie,' Cherokee chief, with twelve or thirteen of his tribe, coming from Houston, camped at Spring Hill, near the house. After tea, we were dancing, when 'Bowie' came in dressed in a breech-cloth, anklets, moccasins, feathers and a long, clean, white linen shirt, which had been presented to him in Houston. He said the pretty ladies in Houston had danced with, kissed him and given him rings. We, however, begged to be excused and requested him to retire, when he in great contempt stalked out, and our dance broke up."

Unrestrained fire was another grim hazard, and even dances were disrupted by threatening conflagrations. For the cowhands, no matter how joyous or how necessary other tasks might seem, looking after the cattle always came first: "When Thanksgiving Day, 1894, came around, for instance, cowboys from Amarillo to Trinidad converged on Channing for a dance. While they were swinging the girls high and stomping the floor hard, word came that a fire had burned off most of the Spring Lake Division, scattering the cattle and necessitating their being herded north to Rito Blanco. Unhappily, but without hesitancy, the hands dropped their partners, put away their drinks, and started out into the chill of late autumn."

In 1900 the XIT boys decided to have a big July Fourth picnic on Hackberry Creek, a running-water stream east of the Cold Water Draw. The event was described in *6,000 Miles of Fence*:

> They had a big barbecue, bread, pickles and coffee for three days. They expected everybody in a hundred miles. They had a "stand" that sold ice cream and lemonade—the first ice cream some of the children had ever seen.
>
> The fireworks were on a wagon bed, and two cowboys who were working for the picnic with more zeal than knowledge started them in the middle of the afternoon. In their excitement they dropped lighted matches in the wagon-bed among the fireworks. A few of the firecrackers went off themselves, then the whole works went to shooting off in all directions. The cowboys had their pant legs on fire; they ran to the creek. Everybody did. It had high banks, but they jumped over them [into the water].

On another occasion, the fire was deliberately set: "I had just finished dancing a jig [and] Jackson was serving hog backbones," related Joe Sappington in a *Frontier Times* article, "when someone yelled out that the prairie was on fire. We all rushed out to save our host's household utensils. We saved two quilts, a box used for a dining table, a skillet, frying pan, two tin cups and a splendid bootjack . . . most everything of any value and the dance went on until broad daylight. A hairlipped fellow who had failed to find a partner had set the prairie on

fire to destroy the house and dancers. Instead, it brought out the heroic character of the men, although some sacrificed most of their whiskers to the flames."

Various pranks at dances helped the settlers keep their sense of humor. A favorite trick involved the babies put to bed in an extra room or the wagons while the parents were dancing. Jokesters would sneak into the room or over to the wagons and exchange the clothing and placement of the babies. Very often the tired parents would not discover until they were many miles away that the child in their child's clothing did not belong to them. Sometimes it was several days before the babies were sorted out and back at home with their parents.

Then there were several saddle tricks to contend with. A cowpoke might stagger out to his pony after the dance to find that the saddle had been turned backward. If the tricksters wanted to create more excitement, they would slip a few cockleburs under the saddle blanket, then stand back to watch the horse pitch and rear when the unsuspecting rider mounted to go home.

One man wrote of what happened after he had won a jigging contest with his energetic rendition of the buck-and-wing, stomping the back step, and the double shuffle. He thought his horse "looked mean" when he threw a leg across the saddle. He knew immediately, when the horse began bucking and threw him off, that something was definitely wrong. The problem proved to be a cow bone shoved under the saddle blanket. He was ready to fight the adversary whom he had beaten in the contest, but the other men held him off. His competitor never did admit that he had put the bone under the blanket.

Students at the Flatrock School in Harper loved to play pranks on the teacher. They would arrive at the school early and dance while one of their friends played a French harp. When they heard the teacher's buggy coming, they'd all slip out the door and run to a nearby creek and hide until she'd ring the bell. Then they'd walk innocently and sedately back into the room.

At a dance in Nueces County, a large wash pot of coffee, surrounded by ample tin cups, was kept boiling under a live oak in the yard. Toward morning, an obliging cowboy had to scrape the bottom of the pot to get a cup of coffee for his partner. Unaware that a tree lizard had dropped into the pot and been boiled, he served it in her cup. She almost fainted when she saw it and promptly threw up. Needless to say, the cowboy had to find another partner.

After a turn-of-the-century dance in the country, attended by a man from town in a high-wheeled Studebaker, the car couldn't pull up the grade out of a creek on the ranch. Cowboys on horses tied ropes to the car anywhere they could and with spirited high jinks accompanied by "six-guns and yells" escorted the man for miles in his "rich man's saddle horse."

Moral Obstacles

"The entrance of a fiddler into a pioneer community was the signal for a shindig, a square dance, or a fiddling contest, and for the disapproval of the church, because the fiddle was thought to be one of the instruments of sin leading the righteous to the paths of Satan." Fiddle lore is extensive. Legends aver that if you dance to the fiddling of an unknown performer, your soul may be in danger. In early America and parts of Europe, the devil was considered the master fiddler.

A few religious leaders vociferously denounced dancing from the pulpit, in books, and in published tracts. They were especially adamant against the waltz and polka, in which dancers "clasped each other in close embrace."

In *The Mathers on Dancing* (1685), a section written by Increase Mather was called "An Arrow against Profane and Promiscuous Dancing Drawn Out of the Quiver of the Scriptures." Another sermon-tract contained the following injunction against modern dancing: "We consider it to be our duty to warn our people against those amusements which may easily become to them an occasion of sin, and especially against the fashionable dances. . . . They throw the sexes into such intimate and voluptuous contact as to excite passion and stimulate indelicate suggestion."

A Methodist circuit rider wrote from the village of Montgomery, Texas, in 1843 that he had gone three-fourths of the way around his circuit and found "nothing cheering, or encouraging, many of the members having backslidden and are spiritually dead—some have been going to dancing school, and some have joined the Baptists!"

A tract written in 1876 listed thirty-five "samples of the fruit found on the tree of dancing," including lasciviousness, suicide, cruelty, infanticide, and assassination. Another, from 1877, stated that "dancing, like gambling, drinking and covetousness, becomes the master passion of the soul," and "when converts join the Baptist church they are expected to give up dancing."

Yet few preachers crusaded against dancing in early Texas, and if they had, they probably would have been ineffective, because only a small percentage of the white population were church members. Pioneer Noah Smithwick tells in *The Evolution of a State* that, after a Bastrop County wedding in 1836, a Methodist minister and excellent violinist, the Reverend Hugh M. Childers, played for part of the dance and even "tripped the light fantastic" himself. "Hornpipes, strathsprays, jigs and reels / Put life and mettle in our heels."

Somehow the idea that the fiddle was

an "instrument of the devil" was extended to include all musical instruments when they were used to play dance music. Thus, when dancing was frowned on too severely by church people, some ingenious dancer loath to give up a pleasurable pastime devised "play parties," although they were not prevalent in Texas before 1846. Actually, one old-timer confessed, the play-party games were modified square dances "done without music to lyrics sung with gusto, if not with melody, while we pranced through the routines." There was a great deal of swinging in these games. Sometimes there was "dancing—with music" in one room at a party, and "play partying—without music" in another. Often, the tantalizing music of the fiddle proved too much of a temptation and a church member would "dance himself out of the church," then he had to be "saved" at the next revival. With some persons it became a habit.

The origin of some of these games is obscure, but most were brought to Texas as part of the cultural baggage of immigrants from Tennessee, North Carolina, Arkansas, and other southern states. Among the games were Skip to My Lou and Little Brass Wagon, closely resembling the Virginia Reel, Old Dan Tucker, Buffalo Girls, and many more. "The tunes were often quite catchy, but the words meant very little and were sometimes sheer drivel":

Mr. Buster, do you love sugar in tea,
Mr. Buster, do you love candy,
Mr. Buster, he can reel and turn
And swing those girls so handy.

"Old Dan Tucker" started as follows:

Old Dan Tucker's down in town
A-swinging the ladies all around,
First to the right and then to the left
Then the one he loves the best . . .

A simple version of the game was played by couples in a circle around an extra man, who represented Old Dan Tucker. The objective was for the extra man to steal another man's partner while the latter was swinging another woman. The man left partnerless became Old Dan and was expected to dance a jig as the couples joined both hands and side-stepped exuberantly around the circle in what was then called "promenading."

Thus, the early settlers dealt with the obstacles, both physical and moral, to insert a note of gaiety and relaxation into the hardship of their lives. They set a pattern followed by many, as they danced across Texas.

6

Country Music Influence

Texans have been called "irreverent and fun lovin'," and Texas music and dances, cowboy duds, and casual lifestyles have long been natural Texas traditions. In the late 1970s and early 1980s, a whirlwind of interest whisked these traditions across the nation and into the public domain, like tumbleweeds before a stiff breeze. Suddenly everybody wanted to play cowboy, and "country" music was at the heart of the cowboy stampede. The music has been known by various names at various times. The popular music, which eventually became categorized as country-western, or country, has been called folk, hillbilly, rural, old-time, mountain, kicker, and barn dance music.

Although the cowboy's reign was short, beginning at the close of the Civil War and ending by the late 1880s, the mores he created have an enduring appeal. The escalation of interest in country music and dance seemed to incite a yearning to experience vicariously the traditional virtues of self-reliance and courage as reflected in the simplicity and freedom of life on the range. The cowboy symbolized courage and guts—the ultimate in manliness—and served as a hero for young and old.

Texas performers played a significant part in developing the form and impact of this type of music, and many Texas singers and musicians helped focus national attention on it. In 1912, East Texan Marion Try Slaughter went to New York to perform. He changed his name to Vernon Dalhart, became the first country music superstar, and produced the first million-selling album. In the 1920s Er-

nest Tubb from Crisp, Texas, one of the first singers to dress like a cowboy, sang "T for Texas" and other songs to make people imagine themselves out on Texas plains. He was one of the first to use an electric guitar on "Grand Ole Opry" and his was the first country group featured at Carnegie Hall. In 1983 he received national honors for his contribution in the field. In Texas he's renowned as the author of the song "Waltz across Texas." Gene Autry, from Tioga, first gained fame by copying the influential Mississippi yodeler Jimmie Rodgers and later developed his own style. Rodgers himself spent his last years in Kerrville, Texas.

Humorist Will Rogers often performed his riding and roping act in Texas. The Sons of the Pioneers, recognized for their version of "Tumbling Tumbleweeds" and "Cool Water," appeared with him at the Texas Centennial celebration. Hollywood promoted country entertainers, including Stuart Hamblen of Kellyville in the "Beverly Hillbillies." Tin Pan Alley went western with "Goldmine in the Sky" and "I'm an Old Cowhand." In the 1930s Tex Ritter, from Panola, became one of the first western performers to gain recognition on radio: "He was a New York sensation." In Corpus Christi, they held "Ritter" dances on the bay front.

In the late 1920s, western swing had already begun its real development with Bob Wills and Herman Arnspiger playing house parties in the Fort Worth area. In 1931 Wills played with the Light Crust Doughboys, a Burrus Mills band, on radio KFJZ. With W. Milton Brown he organized the Musical Brownies in 1933, characterized by the addition of jazz music. Some of their memorable tunes were "St. Louis Blues," "Memphis Blues," and "The Object of My Affection." Wills later organized his Texas Playboys, who became nationally famous. His music featured his heavily bowed fiddle and was characterized by a strong, insistent beat and jazzlike improvisations on the steel guitar: "It was a rhythmic, infectious music designed for dancing."

A trend had started that was to invade the entire world of dance music. At first it was called "hot Texas rhythms"; and later Bob Wills' name became synonymous with western swing and he was recognized as a dominant influence in country music. The man responsible for the twangy, honky-tonk sound has been proclaimed the king of western swing and father of country swing dance.

This son of a Texas sharecropper was raised in a musical family. He learned folk-fiddling from his grandfather, absorbed blues rhythms from blacks with whom he picked cotton, and learned ballads from cowboys on neighboring ranches. His extensive repertory included "One Star Rag," "Rat Cheese under the Hill," "Cotton-eyed Joe," "Ida Red," and "Take Me Back to Tulsa." Jazz numbers, such as "Basin Street Blues" and "Steel Guitar Rag," and black country blues, such as "Trouble on My Mind," were his forte. "You can change the name of an old song," Wills said, "rearrange it and make it swing."

Eventually Hollywood and the movies called him and he appeared in more than a dozen cowboy movies, and the Texas Playboys broke box-office records on the West Coast. After they introduced "San Antonio Rose" in 1938, the leader's famous yell "ah-haa" became a national institution. The colorful band leader–composer–fiddler from Turkey, Texas, had lassoed the emotions of country and western fans across the land. His western swing, a dynamic hybrid of New Orleans jazz, blues, and folk fiddle music kept a Depression populace dancing and left an indelible imprint on the music world. When Wills played, people danced simple couple dances: two-step, the Lindy Hop with a few western twirls, schottische, and Cotton-eyed Joe. Jitterbug arrived in the mid-1930s, but west-

Bob Wills plays as Ann Miller dances on the set of the Columbia movie *Go West Young Lady*, 1941. Courtesy Charles R. Townsend, *San Antonio Rose: The Life and Music of Bob Wills* (Urbana: University of Illinois Press, 1976).

ern styling was smooth and more subdued than that of the east.

During the thirties, several Texas-based factors served to boost the popularity of country music nationally. The Crazy Water Crystals Company of Mineral Wells and other companies used singing cowboys in national advertising. The development of radios, phonographs and Victrolas, and nickelodeons (jukeboxes) created a demand for more phonograph records.

Country-western music exploded during the forties. For example, the "Grand Ole Opry" had 120 entertainers and the "Camel Caravan," sponsored by the Reynolds Company, toured army camps with such entertainers as Eddy Arnold and Minnie Pearl (from Centerville,

Texas). By 1942 they had traveled fifty thousand miles in nineteen states, doing 175 shows for military hospitals. Barn dance programs were played on radio in Cincinnati and Chicago. Dallas had the "Big D Jamboree," Los Angeles had "Town Hall Party," Shreveport had the "Louisiana Hayride," and country music boomed even in sedate New England. Nashville rose to the top. Hillbilly records were popular even in Detroit, where they had migrated with southern workers to "hillbilly" taverns. "Born to Lose" and "You Are My Sunshine" by Bing Crosby were the taproom and tavern classics of 1941. *Billboard* proclaimed Carsen Robison's 1942 "Turkey in the Straw" the most popular hillbilly sound of the year.

America's entry into World War II was the catalyst that made country music a national and, later, an international phenomenon. Defense-work migrations and troop movements instigated the shifting of southern workers and servicemen who sought their favorite tunes wherever they went. During World War II, when country-western bands introduced the kicking and hopping steps of the Cotton-eyed Joe and schottische, along with waltzes and syncopated two-steps, at Texas military bases, the dances acquired the name "kicker dances." When the war ended, country music had infiltrated every section of the nation and many places abroad.

Rock 'n' roll is considered by many to be founded on western swing. Bill Haley and the Comets was the first rock 'n' roll band, and its music became the music of the fifties. Elvis Presley was the "rockabilly" performer who most ably intermingled country music with rhythm and blues in such tunes as "Blue Moon of Kentucky." One of the biggest-selling records of 1959 was the "Battle of New Orleans," by the late Johnny Horton of Tyler. The late Jim Reeves, of East Texas, built a legend in musical history. His velvet singing style brought many new fans

to country music. Waylon Jennings began as a DJ on a local radio station in Littlefield, then became a bass fiddle player for Buddy Holly. Following Holly's untimely death, Jennings created a new sound, which resulted in a record contract and a move to Nashville. After many awards, his "Music Man" went to the top of country charts. He rose to the pinnacle of musical and commercial success, earning Grammys and awards from the Country Music Association.

Willie Nelson came from Abbot, a small farming community where he was raised by his grandparents and picked cotton when young. In 1975, thirteen years after he had his first top-ten hit, "Crazy," his "Blue Eyes Crying in the Rain" made number one and won him his first Grammy for best country vocal performance by a male. He has been a major force in country music, with a long list of awards, including induction in 1973 into the Nashville Songwriter's Association's Hall of Fame, and, in 1979, being named the Country Music Association's entertainer of the year. He has starred in several movies as well.

Kenny Rogers was born near Houston and worked with several groups, including the New Christy Minstrels, before helping to form The First Edition in 1967. After leaving The First Edition, he released the hit song "Lucille" in 1977 and started his climb to fame with fans in the millions, television performances, and movie roles.

Barbara Mandrell of Houston could play the steel guitar at age eleven and soon became proficient on bass, banjo, and saxophone. She was voted female vocalist of the year in 1979 by the CMA and entertainer of the year in 1980. She also starred in her own TV show with sisters Louise and Irlene. Her trademark song is "I Was Country, When Country Wasn't Cool."

Other outstanding Texas performers have found their way to stardom in the wake of those early "gittar pickers and singers" who first broke the regional barriers of country music. They helped spread the "country sound" to the far corners of the world with the force of a Texas tornado.

Al Dean from Baytown recorded the most-called-for version of the Cotton-eyed Joe on his own label, KIK-R. Ray Price from Perryville became a national sensation, and Johnny Rodriguez from Sabinal proved that the country sound is just as sweet whatever the ethnic background of the singer. National recognition has been awarded to Duane Allen from Taylortown, one of the Oak Ridge Boys, and to George Strait with his Ace in the Hole Band from San Marcos. Included on the long list of Texans high on the charts are Mac Davis from Littlefield, Eddie Dean from Pansy, Jimmy Dean of Plainview, Dottsy from Seguin, Freddy Fender from San Benito, Larry Gatlin of Seminole, George Jones of Saratoga, Kris Kristofferson from Brownsville, Roger Miller from Fort Worth, Michael Murphey, Jeannie C. Riley from Anson, Nat Stuckey, Billie Joe Spears of Beaumont, Tanya Tucker from Seminole, Billy Walker from Ralls, Jacky Ward of Grovetown, Gene Watson of Palestine, Don Williams from Floydada, and Johnny Lee of Texas City (who rode onto the national scene as a result of his appearance in *Urban Cowboy*).

Despite the changes in music spearheaded by Presley, the Beatles, protest singers, disco swingers, and new wave rockers, country musicians remained loyal to their own beat. The hippies, drugs, and rebellion of the sixties were reflected in the "do your own thing" solo dances done facing a partner but not touching. Yet old-timers, rednecks, and cowboys never gave up their western swing, two-step, and waltz.

In the fifties and sixties, with the founding of the Country Music Association and the emergence of Nashville as a major recording center, country music became big business. It developed an affinity for the stepped-up rhythms of black music and boogie and blues-guitar styling. The Nashville sound and country-pop music were counterbalanced in the sixties by the honky-tonk and saga songs, the urban folk revival, and renewed interest in traditional country music.

Country-western musicians patiently plugged away while acid rock and disco blasted out in the nightclubs. In the early seventies, an Austin group, Asleep at the Wheel, released its first album of the swing sound that signaled the start of a revival of interest across the country, aided by a revolution in sound technology that made wide distribution and intermingling of diverse musical sounds possible and brought a new and more exciting quality to country music.

In the 1980s the term "country music" embodied bluegrass, rockabilly, gospel, folk ballads, and southern country rock and swing, played with a strong, danceable beat. It was termed "the music of the eighties." In 1979 and 1980, the country music boom resulted in twenty-three gold records. Country music became the second-largest-selling category of recorded music in the United States—ahead of pop, disco, and soul. The number of radio stations programming country music rose from 1,900 in 1969 to 2,403 in early 1980, including 1,534 full-time country stations. More have since switched.

Network television carried twenty-one "country" specials in 1979, featuring such stars as Roy Clark, Johnny Cash, John Denver, Dolly Parton, Kenny Rogers, and Crystal Gayle, and a potpourri from the "Grand Ole Opry" as well as the "Country Music Awards Show." Popular TV series included "The Dukes of Hazzard," featuring a southern theme; "Dallas," with a free-wheeling oil baron star; and the Barbara Mandrell variety show.

Country nightclubs, always popular in Houston and Dallas, expanded. Discos joined the switch, and country-style clubs appeared in unlikely places like New Paltz (N.Y.), Manhattan, Fort Lauderdale, Chicago, Detroit, and Los Angeles. A thousand country-oriented clubs opened in Los Angeles, Orange, and San Diego counties. Sales of country-related clothing and accessories boomed—from high-fashion to discount outlets.

Beginning in 1979 an avalanche of western-style movies helped stampede America into the western era. They included *Electric Horseman, Coal Miner's Daughter, Urban Cowboy, Best Little Whorehouse in Texas, Smokey and the Bandit, I and II, Every Which Way but Loose,* and *Honeysuckle Rose.*

America's renewed interest in dance in general added to the impetus of country-western dancing. Everybody—from dockworker to doctor—got into the act. There was no typical country fan. Above-average earners rushed to dress up in jeans, denim skirts, and ten-gallon Stetsons and kick up their hand-tooled boots in the Cotton-eyed Joe. During the 1980s the country and western theme was popular in Texas at private and public dance parties featuring country music bands. Many invitations to dances for weddings, fund-raisers, and holiday celebrations given by individuals or organizations large and small carried notations on proper costuming: casual western or elegant western. People dressed up in discount-store or designer jeans, calico or expensive suede, cowboy boots of utilitarian or finest leather, straw or felt western hats, and joined the fun.

Many have crooned "Your Cheatin' Heart" or fiddled a lively Texas schottische for the pleasure of the waltzers and kickers on the nation's dance floors. Country dancers make up an impetuous, fun crowd out to have a good time—the music puts them in the mood for it. The country music sound opened up the dance floors to the masses.

7

The Honky-Tonk

Varying terms have been used to describe the type of dancing done at halls where country music was played, such terms as "barn dance," "country-western," "country," "kicker," and "honky-tonk," and this last term, "honky-tonk," has returned to favor as the name of a place where this type of dance is held.

It was honky-tonks, also called roadhouses, taverns, beer joints, juke joints, and dance halls (not ballrooms), that actually put country music on the map during the Depression. Nobody knows exactly where the term originated, but there are various theories. Dictionaries define honky-tonk as a place of amusement offering music, dance, and drink, with descriptive words such as "tawdry . . . cheap entertainment" and "jangling piano music."

At one time black jazz clubs were called honky-tonks, and a song, "Honky Tonk Town," tells of a place "underneath the ground" with "singing waiters, singing syncopaters . . . dancing to piano played by Mr. Brown," who plays "queer, he only plays by ear." In an article, "The Glamour of the Gay Night Life—The Classic Honky Tonk," James Ward Lee says, "The implications of the song are that ragtime or jazz is the music, that Mr. Brown is what used to be called a man of color, and that the establishment—Honky Tonk Town—is operating on the fringes of the law." It has also been suggested that there may be some connection with the idea that the black slang for a white person is "honky." At any rate, despite this early "tawdry" connotation, Depression-era honky-tonks, a cultural phenomenon, came to be "the working man's club, his haven of rest and recreation."

Several factors contributed to the burgeoning of honky-tonks during the 1930s. One was prohibition. When the Eighteenth Amendment was repealed in 1933, Texas was one of the states that opted for the sale of "spirits" to be decided county by county. Even so, counties were limited to selling 3.2 beer. Some counties voted "dry"; others went "wet." County-line taverns sprang up on the wet side of the line to service thirsty customers from the dry side. Another factor was the increasing availability of transportation and a network of all-weather roads. Although new cars sold for around $600, and national annual earnings ranged from $3,382 for a doctor to $216 for a hired hand—providing he could find work at all—many people had a car of some vintage. On a Saturday night a man could check his worn tires for flats, load his wife and kids into his Model A Ford, pull out the choke, and head for the county line for a ten- or fifteen-cent beer or two to wash away his troubles.

Many honky-tonks catered to families, had dance floors, and offered musical entertainment—provided at first by eager local or touring string bands. Aspiring musicians worked by day and picked hillbilly music by night, for little or no pay, just to get the practice. The taverns came to be called honky-tonks, and tunes heard in the relaxing atmosphere included "Driving Nails in My Coffin" and "Honky Tonk Blues." These gave musicians a place to develop their craft, and the honky-tonk became a social institution designed to meet the entertainment needs of small-town folks seeking entertainment. During the last years of the thirties, honky-tonks were everywhere, but nickelodeons, or jukeboxes, had almost completely replaced live music except on weekends.

Jukeboxes were magical music makers

flashing kaleidoscopes of colored lights and moving air bubbles. The first boxes held twelve records, and one side of a Jimmie Rodgers yodeling record could be heard for a nickel. Bigger and better jukeboxes, some holding up to one hundred records, were standardized. Records by the great honky-tonk artists were all the rage. Ernest Tubb sang "Walking the Floor over You," and Bob Wills' toe-tapping "San Antonio Rose" sent dancers to the floor. "It Wasn't God Who Made Honky Tonk Angels" brought tears when sung by Kitty Wells, and Gene Autry inspired romance with "Have I Told You Lately That I Love You."

In 1982 James Lee Ward wrote, "Not much has changed in honky tonks since the fifties, except that parking lots are likely to be paved, the musical equipment is better, and the beer is more expensive. The habitues are still from the same class." He was evidently unaware of the country mania then sweeping the nation.

In a 1981 *Redbook* article, Aimee Lee Ball had recognized the change: "Four years ago, country-western music was the sound of the great unwashed, something for the blue collar man to unwind to. Now it's for everybody and anybody." She stated further that "Texas fever has to do with fantasy, and romance, and the opportunity to borrow from other people's lives," and that "Texas mania goes deeper than media hype. It has something to do with the need to believe in something distinctly American, a proud heritage."

Modern honky-tonk nightclubs of the 1980s have a relaxed atmosphere. The music appeals to the heart and the steps are basic, satisfying, and easy to learn. Time was when country music was a twangy guitar. No more. Now it's a sophisticated, multichannel, well-played, listenable sound that speaks of basic values. The friendly body contact of line and couple positions in such cowboy steps as Cotton-eyed Joe, two-step, western schottische, country waltz, and Texas shuffle are enjoyable for would-be cowboys and cowgirls. Anyone can learn the dances. That is part of the charm that attracts the masses to country dance floors.

During the 1980s, sprawling, monstrous honky-tonks, such as Gilley's in Pasadena and Billy Bob's of Texas in Fort Worth, have emphasized highly commercial side attractions. These include the sale of T-shirts hyping the names of the places and mechanical bulls designed to challenge the ability of the rider to stay on as long as possible before being bucked off onto a pile of mattresses. Even arenas have been incorporated into the complexes, and small rodeos are featured.

Nevertheless, one person has described honky-tonks as "a place where you can let yourself go, be yourself and comfortably meet people—immersed in the spirit of the west."

8

Texas Dance Halls and Clubs

Through the years, dance halls, honky-tonks, and clubs specializing in perpetuating the distinctive dances and customs associated with Texas have sprung up across the state—and new ones keep appearing. Some flourish for a short time, then fade like the last strains of a good-night waltz into historical oblivion. Others retain enough vitality to make a mark, then close down to ghostly silence, to be reactivated only on special occasions, if at all.

A few long-time halls and clubs continue to operate, making concessions to changing times, yet hanging onto enough of their original purpose and selection of dance steps to keep alive the essence of spirited dances and unique traditions that characterize Texan culture.

German Clubs

Nobody does any of the dozens of once-popular elaborate figure formations of the old French dance called a german anymore. Nobody hires a dancing master or conductor to sit in the middle of a seated circle of elegantly dressed couples and call them out to do such figures as Les Petits Ronds, as they did before the turn of the century. Nobody even wears hooped skirts or celluloid collars, or calls dances "germans" anymore.

Yet, dancing groups scattered across the nation and Texas still operate under the name of German Club. In early days they were organized for the purpose of dancing the german. Through the years, though, the german was replaced by new and more popular dances, but in many instances the name stayed on. By the early 1900s, a "german" had become a common name for a large ball or dance that lasted for several hours and included a midnight breakfast.

Dance clubs organized after the early 1900s were also sometimes called German Clubs, although most of the dancers had never heard of the old german figure dance. An old-timer who recalled the many germans held in connection with the University of Texas in Austin incorrectly guessed that they were called germans because of some custom copied from Germany. Many people have erroneously thought the name was used because a particular club was made up of people of German extraction.

Two long-standing examples are the San Antonio German Club and the German Club of Kerr County. They are quite different in concept.

SAN ANTONIO GERMAN CLUB

The San Antonio German Club's elegant affairs highlight the social season in that city. It was founded in 1880 as the Ascension Club by a group of young single men, as was the custom in those days. In early days, they danced the german. As time went on, the type of dancing changed, following trends as new dances became popular.

In 1890 the name was changed to the German Club. During both World War I and World War II, this country's hatred for Germany caused a severe struggle within the German Club, which threatened to destroy it. Many members who did not want to be falsely associated with the German cause sought unsuccessfully to change the name to the Towne Club after Col. L. Towne, a charter member.

In 1936 the San Antonio German Club was chartered by the state of Texas. The charter states that "the purpose for which the corporation is formed is to provide a benevolent and social association to foster good fellowship and the general social welfare and well being of citizens of Bexar County, Texas, and benevolent undertakings generally." The club's bylaws provide that the first of two dances each year shall be called the Opening German, to be given between the fifteenth of October and the fifteenth of November. On that dazzling occasion, reminiscent of the more formal days gone by, the club honors the season's debutantes, chosen by the board of directors (the club has been introducing young debutantes to society for more than one hundred years and shows promise of continuing for another hundred). Twelve persons plus past presidents serve on the board for the club's 600 members. Only 26 new members are selected each year by secret ballot from some 150 proposed by the members. Dues were $120 a year in 1983.

The first Opening Germans were held at the Old Casino Club. Following that, they were held at Turner Hall, and then at the Gunter, Menger, and St. Anthony hotels, and the Villita Assembly Building. The socially elite gathered—and still gather—in tuxedoed and silk-gowned splendor to celebrate the occasion. Beautiful honorees dressed in the latest fashion are formally presented traditionally carrying a bouquet of red roses; then each dances with her father to the sentimental "Thank Heaven for Little Girls."

GERMAN CLUB OF KERR COUNTY

The German Club of Kerr County, which meets in Kerrville, has a different background. It began at a later date than the San Antonio club, so its members never danced the german.

In 1927 Louie and Frankie Real, a German couple, invited a few couples, mostly relatives, to their Hill Country ranch home seventeen miles from Kerrville for an informal dance in their living room. The Mexican American "orchestra" consisted of a guitar and fiddle. The neighbors and relatives had a great time

"shuffling, gliding and hopping" through old-time favorites, such as the waltz, two-step, schottische, polka, Put Your Little Foot, Cotton-eyed Joe, and the "quadrille" (danced in a circle). Later Ten Pretty Girls, "a silly little dance where we stepped sideways this way and that," was introduced.

By popular request the Reals repeated the social. More people joined the festivities, and the crowd outgrew the living room, as well as "scarring the polished hardwood floor." After several months the Reals built a dance hall with a hardwood floor and windows with hinged shutters in a nearby oak grove. The building was built on posts several feet high to catch the cooling breezes and to provide shelter for newly sheared goats and sheep during inclement weather. The hall had a "nap room" for children accompanying their parents. Two more Mexican American musicians, who played guitar, violin, and a clarinet, were added, and a donation was taken up from the dancers to pay them.

Sweet strains of music drifted across the pasture from 8 P.M. to 4 A.M., with an hour out at midnight for sandwiches, barbecue, *cabrito* (goat), and other goodies. Some referred to it as the Turtle Creek Dancing Club. One old-timer told me, "There was seven gates to open on the way, and some of the fellers took a drink at every one, so they arrived at the dance in high spirits." There were also several creeks for the open Model A's to splash across. "We really had to bundle up in the winter," reported one early member, "and there was often ice in the creek water."

A few changes were made in the strict operating regulations in 1934, when the members organized a regular, monthly dance club, with officers, dues, and guidelines for operating the club. At that time it was officially named the German Club of Kerr County, with membership limited to resident couples of the county only. New members were to be inducted through proposal by a member and with the written support of two other members in good standing.

The stated purpose of the club was "to provide refined amusement and entertainment for members in good standing and their guests." The membership was not to exceed sixty couples, membership fee was $1.00 per couple, and the dues $1.00 per month with a $1.50 charge for guests (nonresidents of Kerr County). At first there was a charge for children of members; later, attendance was limited to adults. The dances were set for the second Saturday night of the month, to be held from 9 P.M. to 1 A.M. Dips and snacks provided by a host committee eventually replaced the breakfast. As time went on, a waiting list of ten couples (later upped to twenty-five) was added and dues were raised to $8.00 per month per couple in 1984.

At the time the club became an official organization the dances had been moved to Camp Wabum Annung, now called Camp Chrysalis. It was larger and was six miles closer to Kerrville. As the membership grew, an even bigger place was needed. Otto Schwethelm, a member, invited them to dance on the screened-in porch of his summer home. He later enlarged it and created the Casa de Lomas dance hall "with a good hardwood floor" on his ranch north of Kerrville. The club met there for many years. In 1980 the meeting place was changed to the Knights of Columbus Hall.

The unsealed Casa de Lomas building was apt to be quite warm in summer and a bit chilly in the winter, but it had charm. It was made festive at Christmas with tinsel icicles hung from the bare rafters to cheer the shivering dancers who crowded around the roaring fire in the big open fireplace between dances, and in summer cooling breezes through the open windows were always welcome. Semiformal dress requirements for the winter months called for party dresses for women and suits for men. Summer dress remained informal.

Music for the dancing changed very little after the club's reorganization in 1934; in 1984 the same band, the Highlanders, from Fredericksburg, was still playing for the club. There have been changes in personnel, but several of the musicians remained with the band for more than twenty-five years. A few big band tunes of the thirties and country western songs of later years have been sprinkled between the World War I and old-time dance tunes.

A liberal cross section of the county's residents have been members of the club at one time or another. Ranchers, lawyers, doctors, postal workers, carpenters, teachers, politicians, shopkeepers, barbers, and cowpokes have joined with their spouses in the friendly camaraderie of the Paul Jones mixers and the familiar dances. In 1984 the club had not missed a meeting since its reorganization in 1934.

Sponsored Dances

There are few records of specific dance clubs created by Mexican, Czechoslovakian, German, or settlers of other ethnic groups, but they danced often in connection with their other organizations and meetings.

GERMANIA FARMER VEREIN

One such group was organized in Anhalt in 1860 by a group of German farmers who banded together to protect their stock from hostile Indians and rustlers. In October 1875 it was officially changed to a stock-raisers' club under the name Germania Farmer Verein. Later it changed to a mutual agreement life insurance company with several hundred members.

The Verein Hall was constructed in 1879 and a dance hall was added in 1908. The buildings have served as a social

Ye Days of Yore Dancing Club at the Anhalt Germania Farmer Verein near Boerne, Texas. Courtesy Garland Perry.

center and dance hall from the beginning, and the Verein has a fifty-year-old reputation for Mayfest and Octoberfest celebrations held on the third Sunday of May and October, respectively. Some two thousand persons dance to two bands playing quick-tempo ethnic music and feast on delicious German food served family style.

SAENGERRUNDE

In 1879, German settlers in Austin launched a very active singing society called the Saengerrunde, still going strong in 1984. Under the leadership of a young musical director and band leader, William Besserer, the singers were built into a successful chorus, and later a ladies' chorus was organized. The singers took part in many singing events and sponsored many dances in connection with those events—and they continue to do so.

Some of the dances were staged in Pressler's Garden, and a grand ball held in connection with a very large Saengerfest at the Opera House used an orchestra with forty-three musicians from St. Louis. An early newspaper report stated that on other occasions Austin dancers were lucky to have the Besserer band

available to play for hometown dances. The Austin Liederkranz also entertained with a concert and ball at Turner Hall in 1895. Many such occasions featured dances.

ANSON COWBOYS' CHRISTMAS BALL

A chill "norther" whistled around the corners of the boxlike Morning Star Hotel in Anson, Texas, one dreary December day in 1885. Sand and tumbleweeds rolled down unpaved streets of the little cowtown of two dozen inhabitants. M. G. Rhodes, operator of the hotel, looked out at the bleak landscape and decided to liven things up with a Grand Christmas Ball for the cowhands scattered across the prairie. He circulated the word from one cow camp to another that there would be "great doings" at a ball on the Saturday night before Christmas. He decorated the hall with mistletoe and cedar, and flickering candles lighted the frescoed walls.

The cowhands bedded down their cattle, donned their best Ogden Mills trousers, high-topped polished boots, and best white shirts and loped their cow ponies into town for one "grand sworray [soirée]." Arriving at the hotel they checked their guns and spurs and looked for a partner among the ladies, many of whom had ridden wagon or surrey for many miles. To tunes played on fiddle, tambourine, and banjo, in addition to a bass viol imported by stage from nearby Abilene, they square danced and stepped lively in the Virginia reel, Paul Jones, schottische, and Heel-and-Toe Polka, and sang the words as they swayed and dipped in waltz rhythm to "pretty new shoes" (Put Your Little Foot, or varsouviana). William Wilkenson, nicknamed "Windy Billy," shouted out the calls to the festive gathering.

The ball was such a hit with the cowhands and their ladies that it has been held practically every year since (except during war years). Festivities now take place in a rock building, Pioneer Hall, built just for the occasion by the Texas Cowboys' Christmas Ball Association.

Today, just as in years gone by, men stampede to town in droves for the affair, but they ride gasoline steeds instead of "broncos" and bring their ladies with them. The ball starts with a Grand March, as always, but most of the square dancing has been edged out by modern country and western–type social dancing. Meantime, men dedicated to preserving the cowboy atmosphere wear Stetsons, bright-colored shirts, and cowboy boots, and the ladies glide across the floor in long, flowing dresses modeled after the fashions of bygone years. They still dance to some of the same hoedown tunes that were played at the first ball— such tunes as "Sally Goodin'" and "Turkey in the Straw."

For many years, even after the advent of microphones and public address systems, they followed an old-time custom of having a caller in each square, each calling a different dance. Calls for the "Texas Star," "Grapevine Twist," and "Arkansas Traveller" filled the air. Joyous bedlam resulted in hoarse callers and tired but happy dancers.

The ball was promoted in 1922 by Miss Lenora Barrett in connection with the celebration of the centennial anniversary of Stephen F. Austin's arrival in Texas in 1822, and it was reenacted in the Texas Centennial pageant in Dallas. From time to time participants have taken part in the National Folk Festival, and a group representing the ball danced on the White House lawn in the late 1930s. They went by train and were entertained by the Texas delegation in the House and Senate. Representatives and senators joined in the square dances, schottisches, polkas, and waltzes.

The original lively gathering was made famous by a young eastern poet and reporter who, to conduct business concerning his uncle's ranch nearby, checked into the hotel on the day of the festivities. With an appreciative gleam in his eyes, this nattily attired city man observed while unsophisticated westerners enjoyed folk dance steps always popular in cowboy land. He was William Lawrence "Larry" Chittendon, from the *New York Times*.

Larry later bought his uncle's ranch and aped the cowman's life until the close of the century. He became known as the Poet Ranchman of Texas and wrote "The Cowboys' Christmas Ball" in 1891. The following excerpt describes the scene:

> The room was togged out gorgeous—
> with mistletoe and shawls,
> And candles flickered frescoes, around
> the airy walls.
> And "Wimmin folks" looked lovely—
> the boys looked kinder treed,
> Till their leader commenced yellin':
> "Whoa! fellers, let's stampeed."
> And the music sighin', and a-wailin'
> through the hall,
> As a kind of introduction to "The
> Cowboys' Christmas Ball."

M. G. Rhodes and others who attended the original ball are gone, but hardy pioneers kept coming back annually for

many years to participate in the reenactment. People from every state and from
foreign countries have found their way to
the Cowboys' Christmas Ball to revel in
nostalgic memories.

MATADOR RANCH VALENTINE
DANCE

On the high plains of Texas during the
winter months of the "gay nineties," regular dances were held every other Saturday night, with an occasional extra one,
at big ranches—the Matador, OX, Pitch-
fork, Moon, and McAdams.

One of the most memorable of the big
ranch dances was held February 14, 1895,
at the Matador Ranch in West Texas. The
setting was the headquarters ranch of the
100,000-acre Matador Land and Cattle
Company, established in 1879 in Motley
County, a mile from the town of Matador.
The dance was one of those given occasionally by ranch manager A. J. Ligertwood to keep the cowboys happy and to
promote friendly relations with neighboring ranchers and settlers. Dances were
usually held between fall and spring
roundups, after branding season, when
the men were settled in for the winter.
The guest of honor at the dance was Mrs.
Hicks, the ranch manager's sister, re-
cently arrived from Scotland.

"The grub for the midnight feed is in
the commissary," Ligertwood told the
cowboys, "but how you get it cooked is
up to you." The cowboys rushed to Mrs.
Jack Zurick, who worked there, for assistance. She agreed to get help from the
other women living in headquarters'
residences, and the mess hall cook said
he'd help. They began baking and cook-
ing at once, in preparation for the feast.

The cowboys galloped to neighboring
ranches with the invitations, which soon
included everyone within a radius of
fifty miles. In eager anticipation the men
would drop everything to saddle up and
ride several miles to a neighbor's for a
pound of butter or a few dozen eggs. Fur-

niture was removed from the mess hall,
where the dance was to be held, and the
hall was scrubbed until it shone. A large
bunkhouse was cleared out and long
tables were put up and "laid with white
linens and silver." Then, just as they
thought all was in order for the party, a
heavy snow blanketed everything on the
thirteenth. The cowboys got out the
shovels and spent the day clearing paths
between the buildings.

Among those excited about attending
was Minnie Timms from Matador. "On
the night before," she reported in *Old
Ranches*, "we girls rolled our hair in
curling papers, pressed our best worsted
dress and sateen petticoat; polished our
shoes to a silken sheen, then waited im-
patiently for time to pass. And for once I
was ready on time, dressed in my new
brown cashmere, with a velvet bolero."

In an old stagecoach, she and three
others quickly made the trip from Matador. From the top of a hill they could see
the headquarters layout,

which, against its snowey background
resembled a small village.

Lights gleamed from the white house
and mess hall, glistening across the
snow-packed roadway. The nearby lake
was shot across by a strip of light and
faint glimmers came from several sur-
rounding buildings.

Vehicles were so thick we had difficulty in approaching the house. A
pack of dogs rushed out, barking excit-
edly; from under the machinery shed a
horse neighed shrilly. One of our bays
called back a friendly answer.

But the sounds that thrilled us most
were the clear high notes of fiddles,
coming from the mess hall, mingling
with the thump, thump, of cowboy
boots and the tapping of lighter steps.

The mess hall was dimly lighted with
kerosene lamps in wall brackets with tin
reflectors, and pungent cedar logs crack-
led and burned in a corner fireplace. The

room was crowded and the dance was in full swing, although it was only eight o'clock. Tradespeople, schoolteachers, ranchers, punchers, and their ladies called out friendly greetings. W. P. Gilpin, county judge, was the dancing official. Frank Wilson of Childress and Jeff Morris of Matador played in the orchestra, which was located at one end of the long room. It had been imported from Childress, sixty-five miles distant. The dancers swung into a waltz to the popular tune, "Pride of the Ball." During the evening, the excited young Minnie Timms met her future husband, Benjamin F. Harper.

After the waltz, a big, handsome fellow with a broad smile swaggered into the center of the room. He was Roy McClain, one of the callers. He called out to the fiddler, "All set?" With the fiddler's affirmative nod, Roy's stentorian voice boomed out, "Get yo' pardners for a quadrille." The floor was quickly filled by eager dancers. "S'lute yo' pardner an' let 'er go. / Balance all and do si do."

"The music was quick and devilish," Minnie Timms Harper recalled later, "Buffalo Girls and Billy in the Lowground for the quadrille; Over the Waves and After the Ball for the waltzes." The voice of the caller was melodious and irresistible. "Then such dancing! None of your stately minuets, solemn lancers, or even the giddy waltz could equal it," Minnie declared. Dust rose from the floor about the stomping, prancing feet.

Benches around the room were filled with spectators, neighbors, and friends telling jokes and catching up on the news. Some of the men were apparently just off the range. They wore "battered old Stetsons, rough flannel shirts, chaps, spurs and heavy boots." Most, however, "were slicked up in their Sunday best, shaved, shined, smart looking in their new neckties and handkerchiefs."

Two young men with white buckskin vests encrusted with Indian beadwork in many colors caught the admiring attention of the young women. Others proudly wore watch chains woven of hair from sweethearts or young wives and decorated with gold. Shirt pockets bulged with sacks of "makings" for hand-rolled cigarettes and, "for this occasion, a package of gum." The women were turned out in their best dresses, and the guest of honor "wore a wine colored dress, with steel trimmings. . . . Entering into the spirit of the evening, she was as jolly as anyone there."

During a lull in the square dance movements, a county official's exuberance led him to "show off." He "cut the pigeon wing" and "did the double shuffle, his long coattails cutting queer antics to the merriment of the crowd." "Weave 'em up an' weave 'em down, / Weave 'em pretty girls 'round and 'round," shouted the caller, now a trifle hoarse from his endeavors to make himself heard above the commotion. A happy cowboy let out a whoop, and "Pat Vaughn knocked the back step, to the delight of the cheering crowd. An overjoyous puncher was nabbed by the sheriff and hurried off to sober up."

The long banquet tables were loaded for the midnight supper. The cooks had done their job well. There was roast turkey, ham, chicken with trimmings, and "an endless supply of sweets." Coffee was kept hot in huge pots and boilers.

After supper the old fiddler patted his foot, wagged his head, and played so "fast and frisky" that "only the young bucks could keep step. The floor shook, the lamps trembled, their reflectors threatening to tumble off."

The dance eventually began to wind down with yawns half-hidden, the orchestra taking more time between dances and playing round dances more often. "Finally the mess cook called out: 'It's daylight, let's all have a cup of coffee.' Heavy-eyed cowboys helped visitors with their wraps, while others hooked up the teams." Soon, all the guests were outside in the frosty morning air, shouting farewells. There was one last call from a distant cowboy—and the dance was just a happy memory, never to be forgotten.

"GOING TO CRIDER'S"

As they have on summer Saturday nights since 1925, crowds of blue-jeaned and prairie-skirted dancers and rodeo fans still gather at Crider's. Located in a field west of Hunt, Texas, on a bluff beside the sparkling Guadalupe River, it is miles from anywhere. Toe-tapping country music from a local or imported string band seated on the concrete dance slab mingles in the soft evening air with the last shouts of "Ride 'em cowboy," signaling the end of a rip-snorting regional rodeo that precedes the dance.

Dancers stream from the open-air bleachers and the jam of pickups and Cadillacs in the dusty parking lot to the chain link fence–enclosed pavilion. A cross section of society crowds through the gate under a sign made from a thick rope coiled and curled into the name "Crider's."

Under the stars, cowpokes, capitalists, and campers dance elbow-to-elbow with a common purpose—to enjoy wholesome, down-home entertainment. Status is left in the parking lot. Cowboy boots two-step across the concrete, smoothed by twelve dollars' worth of cornmeal, or kick and hop in a lively Cotton-eyed Joe or schottische.

A young couple dances with a small child held between them while the singer croons about honky-tonk angels; smiling, gray-haired retirees glide smoothly while doing Put Your Little Foot; cowhands in Stetsons waltz with wealthy dowagers; counselors join with their summer campers to romp and stamp in the spoke-line dances; and an oilman twirls his ten-year-old granddaughter in a lively polka. Even a future president, a

governor, astronauts, professional football players, and television celebrities have joined the plumbers, mail carriers, and ranch hands attending. "Saturday night at Crider's is pure Texas," reported a *Houston Post* journalist.

Three generations of the family have worked at Crider's. One would collect and stuff the admission fee into a cigar box—thirty-five cents for men and women free in the early days, up to $2.50 each in 1983. Another stamped the back of each dancer's hand: "Crider's, since 1925."

The Crider family got into the rodeo and dance business on their ranch by accident. It began because "there was nothing much to do" around Hunt, a tiny hamlet near Kerrville in the rolling Texas Hill Country, during hot summer days in 1925. Gradually they built it into an established Texas tradition experienced by thousands of neighbors, campers, and tourists from across the United States.

It began when neighbors rounded up some bulls and goats into the Crider corral to rope or ride for sport. In 1926, Walter and Audrey Crider, owners of the ranch, added a July Fourth barbecue dinner to benefit the Hunt School PTA and a Labor Day "come one, come all" to the festivities then held down on the river bank. In the cooling shade of giant oak and cypress trees, on land owned by the Crider family for as long as anybody could remember, they filled a big ditch with coals, and "Mr. Crow would cook the goat meat."

"Going to Crider's" gradually increased in popularity. After about four years, they built a "plank floor" in a nearby pecan grove and started hiring string bands and having dances lighted by a gasoline generator, following the daytime rodeo and barbecue. More and more people meandered down the country road in Model T's and wagons and on horseback in search of "something to do."

An ebullient local character from a

nearby ranch was known to one and all as "Pappy" Crate. He loved to dance and "show off" with jigs and even headstands on the dance floor. His wife, Willa, preferred playing bridge, so when friends gathered at their house on Saturday nights, Pappy would load up his Model T with the dancers in the crowd and head for Crider's. In those days, no beer or other spirits were allowed in the dance arena, nor did they have restrooms. Pappy contended that there was a continuous line of people leaving during intermission, "headed for the bushes, or to sneak a snort of whiskey from a bottle stashed in a car or wagon." Other restrictions enforced by Mr. Crider were a requirement that men not wear hats while dancing, and that if anyone shouted "bull shit" during the Cotton-eyed Joe, the music would stop. These restrictions were later relaxed, but rudeness or fighting are still strictly taboo.

During the 1920s, summer camps for children began to spring up in the area to take advantage of the inviting setting among huge trees beside water gushing over rock ledges, all conducive to such outdoor sports as hiking, horseback riding, swimming, and boating. The early camps included Rio Vista, established in 1921; Stewart in 1924; Mystic in 1928. These were closely followed by Waldemar, Heart of the Hills, and, subsequently, camps for churches, YMCAs and YWCAs, Boy and Girl Scouts, and others. Eventually, close to three dozen camps were scattered along the river and creek banks and in the wooded hills. This brought an escalating flood of parents and campers to join regulars from the cities who had already discovered the attractive resort setting for their summer cottages—all seeking entertainment.

As the summer camps moved in and tourists began arriving in droves, the Criders increased the number of rodeos, barbecues, and dances. The big flood of 1932 washed away the first platform and

since then the floor has been moved three times and expanded five times on higher ground. Sometime along the way, the barbecue dinners were replaced by a hamburger stand flanked by a small pool hall and restrooms in a metal building, and, as Pappy Crate explained, the lighting was "electrocuted." A rodeo arena was built and expanded as needed. During World War II, with most of the young men away, dancing continued on a smaller scale to music played on a jukebox.

Before Walter Crider died in 1954, he asked the family to work together at running Crider's. His wife, Audrey, worked at it with her sons, Gene and Wilton, and daughters, Elaine Vlasek Hurt and Laverne Moore, until her death in 1982, since which time the sons have carried on.

The present slab is built around a tremendous live oak tree sheltering many tables and benches, where neighbors, friends, and visitors sit to visit or have refreshments between dances. The river side is the most popular, as it catches a cool breeze drifting up over the edge of the bluff. Family members have nostalgic recollections of the large tree. "We used to have a swing in it," recalled Elaine. Gene and Wilton remember that hens roosted in it and goats rested in its shade. It was also where they killed hogs and hung them on the limbs when butchering.

All of the family enjoys dancing, but Wilton Crider and his wife, Bobbie Nell, have gained recognition for their energetic and unique way of doing the old-style Cotton-eyed Joe as a couple dance, rather than in the line formation popular since the 1970s. They have won many trophies for their dancing.

Crider's is part of a past era; it is a simple, unpretentious place where visitors enjoy the age-old dances brought by Texas settlers and integrated into the heritage of the state.

HONKY-TONK DANCE HALLS

A partial list of Texas honky-tonk dance halls includes the following: the Double Eagle and Broken Spoke in Austin, Green Lantern in Monahans, Old Sadie Hawkins in Grand Prairie, El 87 near Comfort, Floore's Country Store in Helotes, Fischer Hall at Fischer, Crider's near Hunt, Twin Sisters at Twin Sisters, Cabaret in Bandera, Luckenbach Hall in Luckenbach, Farmer's Daughter and Texas Star in San Antonio, Kendalia Halle near Blanco, Ponderosa Ballroom in Abilene, Rio Palm Isle in Longview, Red Raider and Cotton Club in Lubbock, a Caravan East in both El Paso and Amarillo, Schroeder Hall in Goliad, and Gruene Hall in Gruene. In Fort Worth are the Pickin' Parlour, Billy Bob's of Texas, Gateway, and Cowtown U.S.A. Among Dallas places are the Longhorn Ball Room and Palms Danceland. Gilley's is in Pasadena, the Long Branch in Kerrville, and the Anhalt Verein Halle in Anhalt.

The appearance, philosophy, age, and size of these honky-tonks vary widely. They range from the simple, down-home country dance halls where home folks and tourists do their courting to big emporiums geared to hyping T-shirts and stressing added attractions, such as mechanical bulls. Some of the halls have been around since the 1800s.

Yet the compelling attraction at all honky-tonks is the music and dancing—the opportunity to indulge in the sheer joy of moving to rhythms and melodies both contemporary and "passed down from generation to generation." They still feature lyrics that "make the world go away," urge a lover to "stand by me," and cajole you to return to the simple life in Luckenbach, where "there ain't nobody feelin' no pain."

Gilley's. Every night and some days, the fiddles wail and guitars twang at Gilley's in that series of metal buildings in Pasadena that grandly calls itself "America's Honky-Tonk," the place where thousands of secretaries, mail carriers, housewives, dock-workers, doctors, lawyers, and senior citizens change into "kickers," or city cowboys and cowgirls, at night. A dirt-floor arena next to the dance hall can seat 7,500 at twice-weekly rodeos. They even sell Gilley's beer and have a recording studio. Mastering the art of riding the mechanical bull before being tossed off onto a pile of mattresses appeals to men and women alike.

It is the place (formerly called Shelley's) where Willie Nelson bombed for $200 in the late sixties and played to a big crowd in 1981 for $87,000. It is the place where in 1971 Mickey Gilley, then a struggling cabaret singer, formed a partnership with the owner, Sherwood Cryer, and the place from which he subsequently launched one of the most successful country-western careers in the land. It is the place where 1980's *Urban Cowboy* was filmed.

Billy Bob's. Another immense, multifaceted, western-hype emporium is Billy Bob's of Texas in Fort Worth—a latecomer on the honky-tonk scene. It has two dance floors, one that features less-famous entertainers. The other, by reservation and with a stiff ticket price, frequently features Nashville stars. There are so many added attractions—mechanical bulls, stands selling T-shirts and gegaws advertising the place, and plenty of handy bars—that it's easy to lose sight of the dancing.

Long Branch. A modern-day honky-tonk with widespread popularity and a down-home atmosphere is the Long Branch dance hall in Kerrville. It's run by a family for families. Marked by good air conditioning, an excellent sound system, and even ramps and restroom accommodations for the disabled, it was launched on family property in 1982 by "Red" and Louise Powell with their children, Billy and Rocky Powell and Earline Grier, and their spouses. "Mother was a country singer and guitar player," Earline explained.

Sometimes called the Long Branch Saloon, the 17,500-square-foot building has a generous 5,000-square-foot dance floor. "The Long Branch is strictly for dancing," Earline said. "We don't cater to the pool players." They've had crowds of up to 2,300 "rootin', tootin'" two-steppers from teenagers to senior citizens gliding to the sounds of such country music stars as John Anderson, Al Dean, Johnnie Rodriguez, George Strait, George Stampley, and Janie Fricke.

Gruene Hall. The German cotton town of Gruene (pronounced Green) in Comal County hosts what they claim is Texas' oldest dance and amusement hall. Gruene Hall was built in 1900 by H. D. Gruene, who established a store at the little town on the banks of the Guadalupe in 1878. Texans now find weekend enjoyment at the fashionably renovated Gruene Hall, although they lean toward rock music as a rule.

Kendalia and Twin Sisters. Kendalia Halle was built in 1903 by a German band club. It was saved from ruin by the present owners, Hal and Karen Morris and Ed King, who reopened it in 1983 with country dances on Saturday nights.

In the tiny town of Twin Sisters, you have to locate a sign that reads "Dance" to find the gravel road that leads to the hundred-year-old wooden dance hall. There for $2.50 you can join the friendly families taking hold of each others' waists for the line dances. You might also see a young boy striding across the floor with a sleeping bag balanced on his head, replacing the old quilt pallet that provided a place to nap while his parents were honky-tonking.

Some of these dance halls have already quietly faded from the scene, but others are still around and new ones have been built. All have left their mark on someone's memory—a moment of enjoyment, a pleasurable escape.

PART TWO
How to Do
Texas Dances

9

General Information

Instructions for dance steps in this book are presented in everyday language to make it easy to learn to enjoy the pleasures of dancing in true Texas country and western style. Many easy-to-follow diagrams and pictures show clearly how each step combination is done and how steps and music fit together. Just follow the step-by-step explanations and you'll soon be dancing the Texas two-step as smoothly as John Travolta did in *Urban Cowboy*.

Clothing

Texas dancing is enjoyable, whatever you wear, but western-style clothing creates an authentic atmosphere and feels the most comfortable while doing the Cotton-eyed Joe kick or a speedy waltz turn. Western pants and jeans are high on the choice list for both men and women. Fabrics range from denim to wide-wale or smooth corduroy to velvet or even satin. In Texas, outfits are classified as casual western for public dances or elegant western for big private-ranch dance parties.

SHIRTS AND BLOUSES

Handsome yoked shirts with pearl grippers come in cotton, flannel, or nylon, in plaids, stripes, or solids for both cowboys and cowgirls. Western ties and bolos give a finished look, but a casual open collar is a popular choice. Denim, suede, or leather vests add a western flair.

Women may opt for print or hand-embroidered full-skirted prairie dresses or skirts of denim or fringed suede. These may be topped with western shirts, lace-trimmed blouses, or vests.

WESTERN TOUCHES

For those who don't want to go the entire western-look route, cowboy touches can be added to a regular wardrobe. A tooled-leather western belt, perhaps monogrammed, adds a nice touch to a favorite outfit.

A felt or straw western hat with a feather in the band adds an authentic accent to either jeans or dresses. A felt Stetson, à la J. R. Ewing or John Travolta, can provide a western accent for even a business suit.

A serious Texas clotheshorse might choose a handsome fitted, western-cut blazer and slacks in suede-trimmed wool or polyester solids or plaids.

BOOTS

Cowboy boots are not a must for Texas-style dancing, but if you've got 'em, wear 'em. They go with everything—menswear, skirts, knit dresses, jeans. Dancers should at least wear comfortable, substantial shoes while doing Texas dances. Spike-heeled sandals or flip-flops aren't too suitable for some of the vigorous steps.

COWBOY HATS

It's not necessary and many people would never do it, but you may dance with your cowboy hat on. There's seldom a suitable place to leave your favorite ten-gallon headgear while you waltz across a Texas dance floor, and, anyway, who wants to buy a handsome, hand-blocked beauty and leave it hiding in a cloakroom?

Manners

After you've learned how to count the beats and determine whether to do a waltz or a polka, you are ready to go dancing. You can put on your cowboy duds and join the fun on some country music dance floor.

Authentic Texas-style manners at the dance are casual but considerate and courteous. High spirits are encouraged, but roughness and rudeness are practically comparable to horse stealing. They won't get you strung up, but you'll definitely be headed off at the pass and shunted into the chute to be hauled off.

WHO ASKS WHOM?

It's acceptable for men or women to casually say to a likely partner, "Let's try this one." Then you and your partner walk out onto the floor, listen a moment until you recognize the rhythm or the tune, take the proper position, and start dancing.

CROWDED DANCE FLOORS

During the dance, if you find yourself hemmed in, do your steps in place until you can locate a clear space and dance your way over to it. Try to avoid collisions—elbowing and fender-bending are definite no-nos. If done accidentally, then of course smiling apologies are in order.

THANKS

When the dance number is over, don't take off like a runaway; head for the sidelines together. Even if your partner wasn't the greatest dancer, a simple "Thanks for the dance" recognizes good intentions, forgives mistakes, and sets the scene for good relations. After all, stepped-on toes aren't duel fodder.

If you especially enjoyed the dance, you can add, "Let's do it again," accompanied by your best smile. It's a good way to get off on the right foot.

Listening and Stepping

To dance to different tunes, you need to be able to determine which steps go with which music. Knowing how to count the beat and recognize the rhythm will help you select the proper steps.

MUSIC BEAT

No matter how complicated the rhythm sounds, you first need to determine whether the music has a three-count beat or a four-count beat. Waltzes have a three-count beat and all others have four-count beats.

If you can count 1-2-3, 1-2-3 in time to the beat, it's time to waltz. If the count comes out 1-2-3-4, 1-2-3-4, then choose another dance step according to the rhythm and tune of the music.

RHYTHM

A few simple guidelines will help you recognize some different rhythms of four-count music. Many country music and easy-listening tunes are played in a smooth rhythm with an even four-count beat, sometimes called foxtrot rhythm. Al Dean, a well-known Texas band leader, calls this even four-count beat rhythm "the Texas shuffle." Old-time fiddled hoedowns also have four-count beats. Some rhythms are played fast and some slow.

The steady, pulsing rhythm of swing music has a lilting, syncopated accent on the downbeat; the polka has strong first and third downbeats; and the schottische has an emphasized upbeat on the fourth count.

STEPS AND MOVEMENTS

Dancing is stepping in time to the beats of the music. It provides the pleasure of that joyous sensation resulting from rhythmical body movement. Sometimes one step is held for the length of more than one beat—a slow step. In addition to steps, there are also dance movements, such as toe touches, kicks, and hops. These add zest to Texas dances.

PATTERNS

Specific combinations of quick and slow steps and movements formed into prescribed patterns are indicated by descriptive terms, such as two-step, step-touch, and step-hop.

General classifications of dance steps are indicated by the rhythm of the music. Three-count step patterns danced to waltz rhythm are called waltz steps. Four-count patterns danced to swing music are called swing steps. Four-count patterns danced to polka music are called polka steps; four-count patterns danced to Texas Shuffle rhythm (foxtrot) are called shuffle steps, and others follow the same design. The same step patterns may be danced in freestyle combinations to any tune having the proper beat and rhythm.

ROUTINES

When an enjoyable series of dance step patterns are combined, establishing a set routine to fit a specific tune, the dance routine is usually known by the name of that same tune.

Sometimes a short routine is danced during the verse portion of a song and repeated during the chorus. Sometimes there is one pattern set to the verse and another to the chorus, making up a routine. In some instances, a routine may also be danced to another tune having the same rhythm.

Popular Texas dances include both freestyle pattern dancing and set-routine dancing.

PARTNERED AND UNPARTNERED DANCES

Partnered dances are those requiring two dancers only, usually a man and a woman. Unpartnered dances are those danced in lines or circles made up of single dancers and without regard to the number of each sex. The line and circle dances have become very popular because many singles flock to the dance floors and feel free to join in the fun without having a partner.

STYLING

No self-respecting Texas dancer would slump while striding across a prairie. Neither should a dancer slump while gliding across the dance floor. Correct styling is the proper use of body position and movement to project enjoyment, attractiveness, and expression while dancing. It is the bounce in the polka, the sweeping glide in the waltz, the light-hearted hop of the schottische, and the exhilarating whirl in the pivot turn.

POSTURE

To achieve good dancing posture—style—dancers should first stand tall with feet flat on the floor about two inches apart. This provides a narrow base and balances the weight. The hips, shoulders, and head should be aligned above the ankles with the head held high and the chin tucked in.

The next step is to tense the muscles enough to hold the position and rise slightly onto the balls of the feet with heels off the floor; then lower the heels until they touch the floor just enough to hold the balance.

In this position a dancer can move forward, backward, or sideward with ease. To create the syncopation and smoothness that are the hallmarks of Texas dancing, the body should move as a firm unit, not like a scarecrow flapping in a field.

When joining hands or arms with others, each holds up the weight of his or her own hands and arms; a good dancer doesn't drag on others.

Getting Going

THE FIRST STEP

Modern Texas dancing leaves a lot of leeway for styling choices, but there are a few rules that absolutely must be followed. One of these involves which foot to begin dancing with.

Taking the first step with the wrong foot might not be as disastrous as trying to mount a horse from the wrong side, but you could easily develop a red face from planting your cowboy boot on someone's foot.

The choice is easy for the man. He should always begin every dance by stepping on his *left* foot first. It's different for the woman, however. She begins with a *different* foot at different times, depending on the dance step routine and the hand hold being used.

In *line formations*, with dancers side by side and facing the same direction, both the man and the woman begin with the left foot.

For *couple dances*, with the woman facing her partner, she must start on the right foot as her partner starts on his left foot. The two feet facing each other on each side must track, as do the front and back wheels of a car. When his left foot moves forward, her right must move backward. When the dance movement goes sideward, the same rules apply.

LINE OF DIRECTION

It's as important to know and follow the proper *line of direction* (LOD) on the dance floor as it is to drive on the correct side of the street. Both are designed to prevent collisions.

The general line of direction movement is counterclockwise. Reverse line of direction is clockwise. That's not to say you must travel in a rigid pattern, as you do on a street. It is more like following the flow of a river that eddies, moves from side to side, or pauses from time to time in a quiet backwater, within the boundaries of its banks. You can dance forward, diagonally, turn around, and back up in line of direction, move toward or away from the center of the floor, and even dance in reverse line of direction (RLOD) for short times in special instances.

LEADING AND FOLLOWING

Once dancers know the proper position, hand hold, and footwork for the dance routine selected, who breaks the trail? Which person gives the signal to start, sets the pace, establishes the length of stride, and decides when to change the step? In other words, who leads or guides, and who follows?

Time was when the man demanded that he be honored (or saddled) with this responsibility. The woman had no choice but to follow his lead the best she could—whether he galloped across the floor out of step with the rhythm being played, or whether his performance was limited to a jerky, one-sided lope. On the sly, a woman having more dance skills sometimes provided a tactful guiding push or pull here and there to an often grateful partner—just as long as the help wasn't obvious.

Nowadays, it's acceptable for the one who knows the steps—whether the man or the woman—to take the lead tactfully for the other to follow. And why not? It makes for more interesting and enjoyable dancing.

Usually, however, as soon as the man learns the routine, he takes the lead by combining firm, but gentle (never obvious) pushes and pulls. The leader should move assertively, and the follower should alertly duplicate the countermovements, much as you go through a revolving door by synchronizing your movement to the speed of its turning.

Dance Positions

COUPLE: CLOSED POSITION

The most popular dance position for couples is the traditional one using the waist-hand (ballroom) hold (see fig. 1). Introduced years ago, it hasn't yet been improved on. A man and a woman stand very close, facing each other. His right toe should point between her feet, and her right toe should point between his

1. Closed position, waist-hand (ballroom) hold

2. Semiclosed position, waist-hand (ballroom) hold

3. Open position, shoulder (varsouviana) hold

feet. This slightly off-center position keeps the feet from colliding and allows each dancer to watch out for collisions over the other's right shoulder.

COUPLE: SEMICLOSED POSITION

A dance routine calling for this position sometimes alternates between closed and semiclosed positions. Starting with the closed position and using a waist-hand (ballroom) hold, the dancers open away from each other forming a V shape with their bodies (see fig. 2). The waist-hand (ballroom) hold is loosened on the open side to permit this movement.

COUPLE: OPEN POSITION

A man and a woman stand side by side with the woman at the man's right, their hands and arms positioned in a shoulder hold, also called varsouviana hold (see fig. 3). This hold allows the woman to dance across in front of the man to his left side, and back, without releasing hands.

DRILL LINE: NO HOLD

Two or more dancers stand side by side, facing the same direction in no-hold lines when dancing rock crossover dances (see fig. 4). Dancers do not touch each other in this position. Any number of people may make up a no-hold line, and several lines may stand one behind the other across or down the floor, since each dancer stays in approximately the same place during the dance. Dancers must watch to keep in alignment with each other, however. They hold their hands in rock position.

COUPLE: FACING

Couples in facing position stand about a foot apart with hands in no-hold or handclasp position (see fig. 5).

CIRCLE

Dancers facing inward to form a circle should try to keep the formation round and remain equidistant as they circle around. They use the handclasp hold (see fig. 6).

4. Drill-line, rock position, no hold

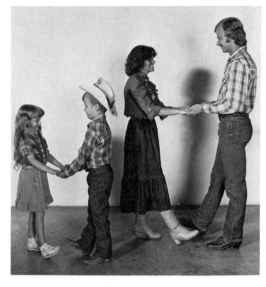

5. Facing position, handclasp hold

SPOKE-LINE, WAIST HOLD

Two to seven persons in any combination of male and female make for comfortable dancing in a line using waist holds (see fig. 7). Waist-hold lines should be positioned like spokes in a wheel extending from a hub in the center of the floor. The dancers' movement around the hub resembles a large wheel turning on its side.

Holds

WAIST-HAND (BALLROOM) HOLD

The waist-hand hold (also known as the ballroom hold), is used by couples in closed and semiclosed positions. The man's right arm firmly encircles the woman's body slightly above the waist, with the palm of the hand against the center of her back near the bottom of her rib cage (see fig. 1). (If the hand is held too high, it pulls her off balance.) This arm holds the couple together, and hand pressure is used to guide the woman into turns or into dancing forward when the man backs up.

The woman's left hand rests lightly on the man's right shoulder with her forearm lying along his upper arm so she can use the feel of his arm and shoulder movements as a guide to following his movements and to steady herself at the right distance for comfortable dancing.

The man's left arm, held slightly curved, is extended sideward with palm up; the woman puts her right hand in his left, palm down. Arms and hands should be held relaxed, but ready to tense when needed for guiding or following into step or direction changes. In the semiclosed position, the arm holds are altered slightly to allow dancers to open into a V position on either side (see fig. 2).

SHOULDER (VARSOUVIANA) HOLD

A man and a woman stand side by side with the woman at the man's right side. The woman holds her hands up at about shoulder height on each side, palms forward. The man reaches his right hand behind her shoulders and grasps her right hand with his palm around the

6. Circle position, handclasp hold

7. Spoke-line position, waist hold

back of her hand and his fingers curled into her palm, making sure not to lean on her shoulders. He reaches his left hand across his own chest and joins it, palm facing hers, with the woman's left hand, palm facing forward. The woman supports the weight of her own arms and does not pull down on the man's hands (see fig. 3).

NO-HOLD, ROCK POSITION

In no-hold couple or line dancing the dancers do not join hands, but hold them in rock position, as follows. The man hooks his thumbs in his pockets or under his belt at each side of his waist. If wearing a skirt, the woman grasps it at the sides and fans or flares it forward and backward while dancing (see fig. 4). If she is wearing jeans, she uses the same hand position as the man.

HANDCLASP HOLD

The handclasp hold is used by a couple or a circle of people facing each other (see figs. 5 and 6). The men hold out

their hands palms up, and the women join hands with them, palms down, right hands in left. The arms should be slightly curved and held at a comfortable height just above the woman's waist. Each person supports the weight of his or her own hands.

WAIST HOLD

In line dances, two or more dancers stand side by side using a waist hold (see fig. 7). Arms are placed in a loosely held (no clutching), friendly hug around each other's waists to keep the line straight and to help establish a common gait. The dancers on each end of the line may join their free hands with the one around their waists, or women may flare their skirts with the free hand.

Diagram Symbol Chart

The simple and easy-to-learn symbols on this chart are guidelines to understanding the step-by-step instruction diagrams accompanying each dance pattern or routine included in the twenty-two Texas dances described in the following pages. The symbols indicate clearly such specifics as whether the dancer should step with weight on the full foot or only the ball of the foot; when to touch the heel or toe to the floor; whether to dance forward, backward, or sideward; how many counts each step takes. Note: In the illustrative dance-step diagrams, the space between steps is sometimes increased in the interest of clarity.

Legend

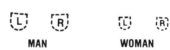

movement forward, sideward

movement backward

turning movement forward

turning movement backward

R   right foot

L   left foot

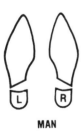 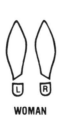

MAN   WOMAN

full foot, solid line: weight on entire foot

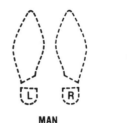

MAN   WOMAN

full foot, broken line: full foot touching floor with no weight on it

MAN   WOMAN

ball of foot only, no heel, solid line: weight on ball of foot

MAN   WOMAN

ball of foot only, no heel, broken line: touch ball of foot on floor with no weight on it

MAN   WOMAN

heel of foot only, broken line: touch heel only, with no weight on it

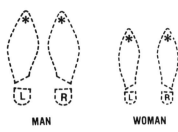

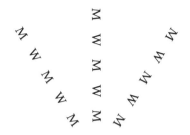

MAN   **WOMAN**

*full foot, broken
line, asterisk on
toe: foot raised,
as in a kick, or
crossed over
other foot*

spoke-line formation

W	M	W	W
M	M	W	M
W	M	M	W
W	M	W	M

*footprint overlaying
another one: two steps
taken in the same place*

drill-line formation

M *(man)* W *(woman)*

Numerals: *numbers placed inside or
near footprints indicate the sequence of
the steps and how long to hold the position; extra numbers within parentheses
denote how much longer to hold the
position for the extra counts.*

*line of dance direction
(LOD)(counterclockwise)*

*reverse line of dance direc-
tion (RLOD) (clockwise)*

*Start: unnumbered footprints labeled
START indicate the foot or feet placement before beginning the actual steps
of the routine.*

Example:

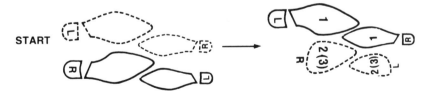

*start with feet side by side, weight on
man's right foot, woman's left foot;
other foot on floor, no weight*

*man steps forward on left foot (woman
backward on right foot)—count 1; man
touches ball of right foot beside left foot
(woman touches ball of left foot beside
right foot)—count 2, 3*

10

Texas Dances

COTTON-EYED JOE

The Dance Format

The format for the dance descriptions includes up to ten parts used on a selective basis as appropriate for the specific type of dance. These parts, with explanatory and reference notes, are listed below:

Name of dance
Introduction
Record(s): examples are listed
Position: see Dance Positions, page 66; Holds, page 68
Footwork: *same*—all dancers use the same foot for the steps; *opposite*—partners use opposite feet for the steps
Step arrangement: see Routines, page 65; Patterns, page 65
Formation: see Diagram Symbol Chart, pages 70–71
Steps: step patterns and routines are divided into steps, each of which is described separately; cross references are also given to specific dances
Diagrams and photographs accompany appropriate dance descriptions

In Texas Hill Country styling for this popular dance, the cross-lift and kick-step are smoothly controlled. One cowgirl said to me, "If you can raise your boot too high, your jeans aren't tight enough."

A line routine and a couple routine are given here, but feel free to kick up your heels and improvise if the spirit moves you.

Spoke-line Routine

Records: Any Cotton-eyed Joe; for example, KIK-R label, K-202-A; LP 10012; KIK-R, LP-10013
Position: Spoke-line, waist hold
Footwork: Same
Step arrangement: Routine (verse, chorus)

STEPS
Pattern 1, verse: cross-lift, kick, back up
   1. Cross-lift left foot in front of right knee—count 1(2) (*variation:* kick instead of doing the cross-lift). Shout, "Whoops."

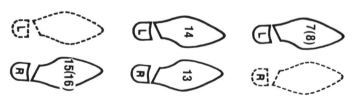

Pattern 1
Spoke-line, kick-step, and back up routine

Spoke-line cross-lift step

Spoke-line kick-step

2. Kick left foot forward—count 3(4). Shout, "Whoops," again.

3. Step left foot backward—count 5.

4. Close right foot backward beside left foot—count 6.

5. Step left foot backward—count 7(8).

Repeat above routine using opposite footwork. Begin with cross-lift right foot in front of left knee—count 9–16.

Repeat entire sequence.

Pattern 2, chorus: two-steps
Beginning with left foot, take eight two-steps forward (see Two-Step, line, p. 109).

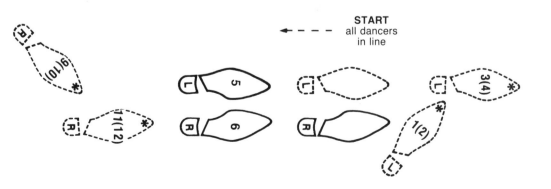

After heel-and-toe polka, ready to turn away into separate two-step circles

Couple circle two-step away from each other after the polka steps

Couple Routine

Records: Same as for spoke-line routine
Position: Couple, closed, semiclosed hold
Footwork: Opposite; step directions given for man
Step arrangement: Routine (verse, chorus)

STEPS
Pattern 1, verse: Heel-and-Toe Polka, sideward

1. Heel-and-toe polka step toward man's left (woman's right) (see Heel-and-Toe Polka, couple, semiclosed, closed, p. 87).

2. Heel-and-toe polka step toward man's right (woman's left).

3. Heel-and-toe polka step toward man's left (woman's right).

4. Heel-and-toe polka step toward man's right (woman's left).

Pattern 2, part A, chorus: Circle Two-Step

After pattern 1, release hold, both turn and two-step away from each other (see Two-Step, line, p. 109). Man starts on left foot and circles to the left. Woman starts on right foot and circles to the right. On the fourth two-step, they should have completed the circle and be back in original position facing each other. The fourth two-step may take the form of stamp, stamp, stamp.

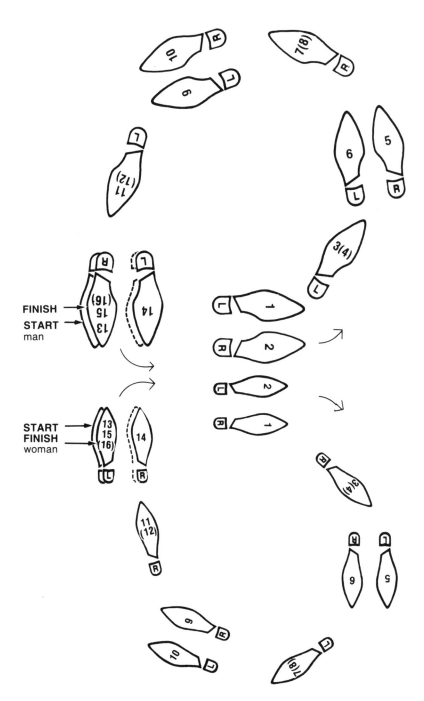

Pattern 2, part A
Couple circle two-step routine

Couple push-step routine

Pattern 2, part B, chorus: push-step

Partners, now facing, take a waist-hand (ballroom) hold (*variations*: two-hand hold; no hold, with thumb on one hand extended in direction moving, as if thumbing a ride). Moving toward the man's left (woman's right), both dancers do four push-steps, then reverse direction to do four push-steps toward the man's right (woman's left), returning to place. *Variation*: substitute eight turning two-steps in waist-hand hold, closed position for the push-steps (see Two-Step, turn, p. 113).

In the push-step, both feet move at practically the same time in opposite sideward directions.

1. To push-step to the left, man starts with weight on the right foot and pushes with the ball of the right foot, simulta-

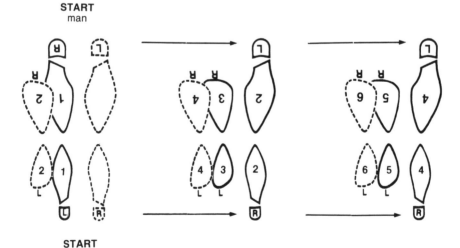

Pattern 2, part B
Couple push-step to man's left

neously lunging sideward to the left to land on the left foot. Upon landing, the ball of the right foot slips and lifts as if it loses traction.

2. For the next push-step, the man puts weight on the ball of the right foot (the one that slipped) and pushes, again simultaneously lunging sideward to the left to land on the left foot. Reverse the foot action to push-step to the right.

Repeat entire dance routine to end of music.

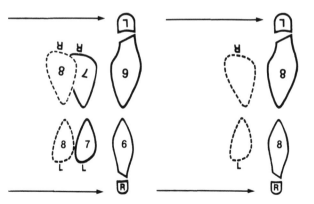

COWBOY POLKA (JESSIE POLKA)

Spirited dancers increase their fun by seeing how far they can lean, keeping the body in straight alignment, while extending one foot forward or backward for a heel or a toe touch.

Records: Any polka; for example, *Jessie Polka*, MacGregor No. 5001B; Blue Star No. BS-1588-A
Position: Spoke-line, waist hold; couple, shoulder (varsouviana) hold
Footwork: Same
Step arrangement: Routine (verse, chorus)

STEPS
Pattern 1, verse: heel-step, toe-touch, heel-and-toe
1. Touch left heel forward—count 1.
2. Step on left foot beside right foot—count 2.
3. Touch right toe backward—count 3.
4. Lift right toe slightly and touch backward again—count 4.
5. Touch right heel forward—count 5.
6. Step on right foot beside left foot—count 6.
7. Touch left heel diagonally forward to the left—count 7.
8. Cross-touch left toe in front of right toe—count 8.

Pattern 2, chorus: two-steps
Beginning on left foot, do four two-steps forward in line of dance direction (see Two-Step, line, forward, p. 109).
Variation: a couple may change to closed, waist-hand (ballroom) hold for the two-steps (see Two-Step, couple, pp. 110–111).
Repeat entire dance routine to end of music.

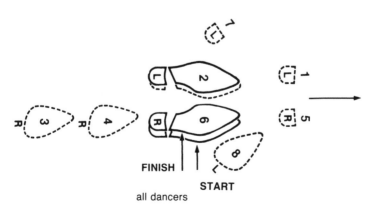

FINISH   START
all dancers

Pattern 1
Spoke-line heel-step, toe-touch, heel-and-toe routine

Toe-touch backward

Heel-touch diagonally forward to left

Cross-touch left toe

DOUBLE SHUFFLE

The Double Shuffle combines sideward two-steps with side-touch steps.
It is not to be confused with the Texas
Shuffle step. It may be danced with a
wide range of styling: flex the knee on
even-numbered beats to swing rhythm;
stamp on the first and third beats to
polka music. Some people dance pattern
1 only and some dance pattern 2 only.

Record: Any four-count beat music
Position: Couple, waist-hand (ballroom)
hold
Footwork: Opposite; step directions
given for man
Step arrangement: Pattern

STEPS
Pattern 1: side-step, touch-step
1. Man steps left foot sideward to
left—count 1(2).
2. Man touches right toe beside left
foot—count 3(4).

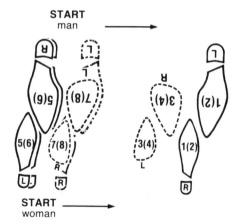

Pattern 2
Couple side-step, touch-step routine

3. Man steps right foot sideward to
right—count 5(6).
4. Man touches left toe beside right
foot—count 7(8).

Pattern 2: side two-step
1. Man steps left foot sideward to
left—count 1.
2. Man steps right foot sideward to
left, beside left foot—count 2.
3. Man steps left foot sideward to
left—count 3(4).
4. Man steps right foot sideward to
right—count 5.
5. Man steps left foot sideward to
right, beside right foot—count 6.
6. Man steps right foot sideward to
right—count 7(8).

Repeat patterns 1 and 2 to end of music.

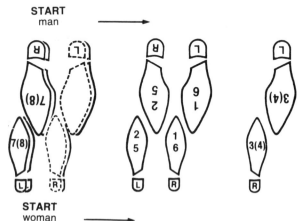

Pattern 1
Couple side two-step routine

GARDEN WALTZ

The Garden Waltz has two parts, each with a different rhythm. It is unique in that the waltz is performed in a spoke-line made up of one man between two women. They use waist holds for the waltz steps, and for the polka (or two-step or one-step) part, the man forearm swings each woman in turn.

Forward waltz

Record: *Garden Waltz*, Bellaire, 5031-A (LH-1887)
Positions: Spoke-line (a man between two women), waist hold; no hold, women facing man between them
Footwork: Same
Step arrangement: Routine (waltz, two-step, or polka)

STEPS
Pattern 1: waltz
   A man and two women, one on each side of him, begin with their left feet and dance twelve waltz steps forward in line of dance direction (see Spoke-line Waltz—forward steps only, p. 115). Some dancers prefer the slow or hesitation waltz step (see Waltz, slow, pp. 120–121).

Pattern 2: polka or two-step or one-step
   Dancers release their waist holds and the women face the man between them. Using a fast polka or two-step (see Two-Step, line, p. 109) or a one-step (see One-Step, quick, pp. 94–95), and starting with the left foot, the man alternates between turning the woman at his right with a right forearm grasp, and the other woman with a left forearm turn, making a figure eight around them. He turns each woman four times. The women do whatever step he chooses to do. *Dancers continue alternating the waltz and polka, or two-step, patterns to end of music.*

Forearm swing

FREEZE

In the Freeze, the dancers turn right to face each of the four directions during the dance: north, east, south, and west.

Since the step pattern resembles the schottische, it is popular both as a spoke-line dance and as a couple dance using a shoulder (varsouviana) hold in open position, instead of no-hold lines. The man takes a longer step on the turns to keep the woman at his right side.

It is a fun dance marked by an occasional surprise challenge when someone shouts, "Freeze, 2, 3, 4," on the step in which dancers rock forward, and everyone freezes in that position for the four counts.

Record: Any medium-speed rock rhythm
Position: Drill-line, no hold, rock hand
    position
Footwork: Same
Step arrangement: Routine

STEPS
Fig. A
    1. Step left foot sideward to left—count 1.

Rock forward on right foot and freeze

2. Step right foot sideward to left in back of left foot—count 2.

3. Step left foot sideward to left—count 3.

4. Cross-lift right foot in front of left knee—count 4.

Fig. B
5. Step right foot sideward to right—count 5.

6. Step left foot sideward to right in back of right foot—count 6.

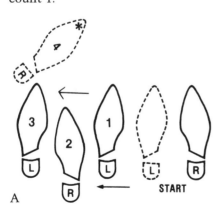

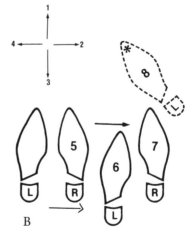

A

B

Freeze routine

Rock backward on left foot

After pivot-turn to right

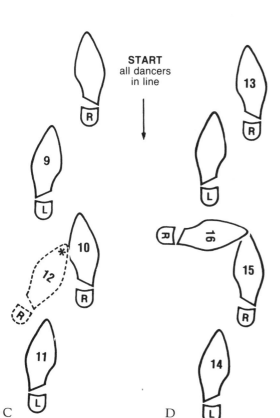

C   D

7. Step right foot sideward to right—count 7.

8. Cross-lift left foot in front of right knee—count 8.

Fig. C

9. Step left foot backward—count 9.

10. Step right foot backward—count 10.

11. Step left foot backward—count 11.

12. Cross-lift right foot to front of left knee—count 12.

Fig. D

13. Step right foot forward, bend knee, and rock (lean) forward—count 13.

Note: This is the point at which the leader (someone with a loud voice) occasionally calls out "Freeze, 2, 3, 4." Dancers hold this forward rock position for the four counts, then continue the dance.

14. Step left foot backward and rock backward over it, lifting right foot—count 14.

15. Step right foot forward—count 15.

16. Pivot one-quarter turn to the right on ball of right foot—count 16.

Repeat entire dance routine to end of music.

FOUR CORNERS

Cross-lift right foot

In Four Corners, the dancers turn left to face each of the four directions: north, west, south, and east.

Record: Any medium-speed rock rhythm
Position: Drill-line, no hold, rock hand position
Footwork: Same
Step arrangement: Routine

STEPS
Fig. A
   1. Touch left heel forward—count 1.
   2. Step on left foot—count 2.
   3. Touch right heel forward—count 3.
   4. Step on right foot—count 4.

Fig. B
   5. Stand on balls of feet and spread heels—count 5.
   6. Close heels—count 6.

Fig. C
   7. Spread heels again—count 7.
   8. Close heels and take weight on them—count 8.
   Repeat steps 1–8—count 9–16.

Fig. D
   9. Touch right heel forward—count 17.
   10. Touch right toe in front of left toe—count 18.
   11. Touch right heel forward—count 19.
   12. Step on right foot—count 20.

Fig. E
   13. Touch left heel forward—count 21.
   14. Touch left toe in front of right toe—count 22.
   15. Touch left heel forward—count 23.
   16. Step on left foot—count 24.

Fig. F
   17. Step forward on right foot—count 25.
   18. Kick left foot forward—count 26.

Fig. G
   19. Step left foot backward—count 27.
   20. Touch right toe beside left foot—count 28.
   21. Step on right foot toed-in across left foot, making a one-quarter turn to the left—count 29.
   22. Step on left foot beside right foot—count 30.
   23. Step right foot backward—count 31.
   24. Touch left toe backward—count 32.

   Repeat entire dance routine until end of music.

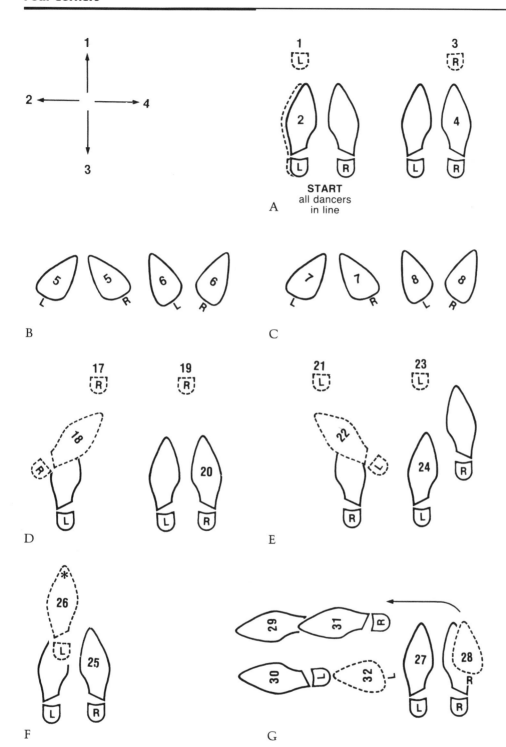

Four Corners routine

HEEL-AND-TOE POLKA

Touching the heel and the toe between the energetic polka two-steps gives dancers a breather and adds variety. Two of the many versions of this combination as danced by Texas couples are described here—one in open position, the other in closed position.

Cross-touch left toe in front of right toe

Couple, Open Position

Record: Any polka
Position: Couple, open, shoulder (varsouviana) hold
Footwork: Same
Step arrangement: Routine (verse, chorus)

STEPS
Pattern 1, verse: Heel-and-Toe Polka step

1. Touch left heel diagonally forward to left—count 1(2).

2. Cross-touch left toe in front of right toe—count 3(4).

3. Step left foot forward—count 5.

4. Step right foot forward beside left foot—count 6.

5. Step left foot forward—count 7(8). (*Optional*: left foot hop on count 8.)

Repeat steps 1–5 on opposite feet—count 9–16.

Repeat entire sequence.

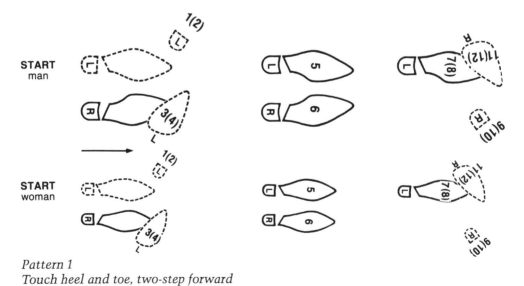

Pattern 1
Touch heel and toe, two-step forward

Touch heel to side

Touch toe beside supporting foot

Pattern 2, chorus: polka two-steps
Beginning with left foot, take eight polka two-steps forward (see Two-Step, Polka Two-Step, line, forward, p. 109).

Couple, closed position

Record: Any polka
Position: Semiclosed, closed
Footwork: Opposite, step directions given for man
Step arrangement: Routine (verse, chorus)

STEPS
Note: A couple in closed position with waist-hand (ballroom) hold opens side-to-side to semiclosed positions during the dance.

Pattern 1, part A
Semiclosed position, open V to man's left:
1. Man touches left heel sideward to left—count 1(2).
2. Man cross-touches left toe in front of right toe—count 3(4).
Closed position:
3. Man steps left foot sideward to left—count 5.
4. Man steps right foot sideward beside left foot—count 6.
5. Man steps left foot sideward to left—count 7(8).
(*Optional*: left foot hop on count 8.)

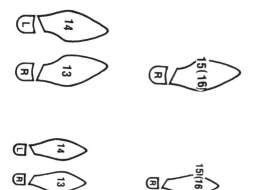

Pattern 1, part B

Semiclosed position, open V to man's right:

1. Man touches right heel sideward to right—count 1(2).

2. Man cross-touches right toe in front of left toe—count 3(4).

Closed position:

3. Man steps right foot sideward to right—count 5.

4. Man steps left foot sideward beside right foot—count 6.

5. Man steps right foot sideward to right—count 7(8).

(*Optional*: right foot hop on count 8.)

Pattern 2, chorus: polka two-steps

Beginning with man's left and woman's right foot, do eight turning polka two-steps (see Polka Two-Step, left turn, pp. 113–114).

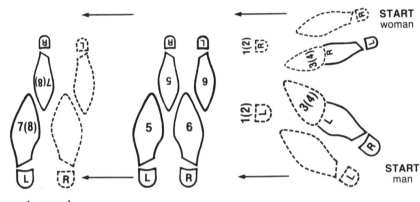

Pattern 1, part A

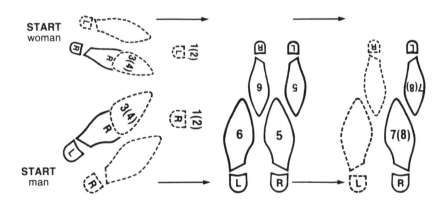

Pattern 1, part B
Touch heel and toe, two-step sideward

HERR SCHMIDT

This dance may be performed either in a circle formation or by a couple.

Circle

Record: *Herr Schmidt*, SARG, 222:45
Position: Circle, handclasp hold
Footwork: Same
Step arrangement: Routine (verse, chorus)

STEPS
Pattern 1, part A, verse: hop/heel-touch step
This pattern is danced while holding hands in a circle.

1. Simultaneously: hop on right foot and touch left heel forward—count 1(2).

2. Simultaneously: hop onto left foot and touch right heel forward—count 3(4).

3. Simultaneously: hop onto right foot and touch left heel forward—count 5.

4. Simultaneously: hop onto left foot and touch right heel forward—count 6.

5. Simultaneously: hop onto right foot and touch left heel forward—count 7(8).

Pattern 1, part B
1. Repeat steps 1–5, using opposite feet.

Repeat parts A and B.

Pattern 2, chorus: circle left and right, galop step
The galop step consists of stepping sideward with one foot and quickly stepping beside it with the other foot in a galloping motion.
Circle left:
1. Step left foot sideward to left—count 1.

Hop, heel-touch

2. Quickly step right foot left beside left foot—count 2.

3. Step left foot sideward to left—count 3.

4. Quickly step right foot sideward to left beside left foot—count 4.

5. Step left foot sideward to left—count 5.

6. Quickly step right foot sideward to left beside left foot—count 6.

7. Step left foot sideward to left—count 7.

8. Touch ball of right foot beside left foot—count 8.
Circle right:
1. Repeat steps 1–8, using opposite feet—count 9–16.

2. Repeat steps 1–16.

Repeat patterns 1 and 2 to end of music.

Hop, heel-touch

Forearm swing

Couple Routine

Record: *Herr Schmidt*, SARG, 222:45
Position: Couple facing, handclasp hold,
   forearm swings
Footwork: Same
Step arrangement: Routine (verse,
   chorus)

STEPS
*Pattern 1, part A, verse: hop/heel-touch
step*

1. Simultaneously: man hops on right
foot and touches left heel forward as
woman also hops on her right and
touches left heel forward—count 1(2).

2. Simultaneously: man hops onto left
foot and touches right heel forward as
woman also hops on her right and
touches left heel forward—count 3(4).

3. Simultaneously: man hops onto
right foot and touches left heel forward
as woman also hops on her right and
touches left heel forward—count 5.

4. Simultaneously: man hops onto left
foot and touches right heel forward as
woman also hops on her right and
touches left heel forward—count 6.

5. Simultaneously: man hops onto
right foot and touches left heel forward
as woman also hops on her right and
touches left heel forward—count 7(8).

*Repeat steps 1–5 three more times
(four in all).*

Pattern 2, chorus

1. Partners change handclasp to right
forearm grasp. Beginning with left foot,
both man and woman take eight one-
steps or two-steps in clockwise direction, at the same time swinging each
other around (see Two-Step, p. 109, and
One-Step forward, pp. 94–95).

2. Change to left forearm grasp. Swing
in counterclockwise direction for eight
steps.

Repeat steps 1 and 2.

*Repeat entire sequence three more
times (four in all).*

*Repeat patterns 1 and 2 to end of
music.*

MEXICAN POLKA

Grapevine step

The grapevine pattern, one of the many steps danced to *conjunto* music, is shown here. Other steps may be combined with the grapevine.

Record: Any *conjunto* polka
Position: Couple, closed, waist-hand (ballroom) hold
Footwork: Opposite; step directions given for man
Step arrangement: Pattern

STEPS
Pattern 1, part A: grapevine to man's left

If using a waist-hand (ballroom) hold, the hold should be loosened to allow more space between partners.

1. Man steps left foot sideward to left—count 1.

2. Man crosses right foot sideward to left in front to other side of left foot—count 2.

3. Man crosses left foot sideward to left in back to other side of right foot—count 3.

4. Man crosses right foot sideward to left in back to other side of left foot—count 4.

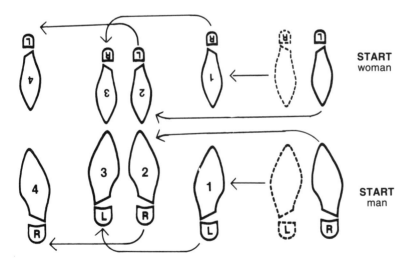

Pattern 1, part A
Grapevine step

Pattern 1, part B: grapevine to man's right

1. Man crosses left foot sideward to right in front to other side of right foot—count 1.

2. Man crosses right foot sideward to right in back to other side of left foot—count 2.

3. Man crosses left foot sideward to right in back to other side of right foot—count 3.

4. Man crosses right foot sideward to right in front to other side of left foot—count 4.

Note: Other step patterns for couples that may be combined extemporaneously with the grapevine are described under Two-Step (pp. 110–111), One-Step (pp. 94–95), Heel-and-Toe Polka (pp. 87–88), and Texas Shuffle (pp. 106–107).

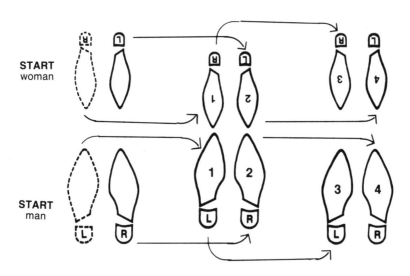

Pattern 1, part B
Grapevine step

MIXER DANCES

Mixers are dance routines designed to break the ice at a social and help people get acquainted by providing exchanges of partners. At a given signal, such as a simple shout to change partners, blowing a whistle, or ringing a bell, the dancers change partners. The Paul Jones, Popcorn, and Snowball are all tried-and-true Texas mixer dances.

Paul Jones

When a Paul Jones is announced, the band plays a snappy tune, usually a one-step, that starts couples dancing. After several measures, the leader blows a whistle or otherwise signals for the dancers to form two concentric circles, with the women dancing single file clockwise around the inside, men single file counterclockwise around the outside circle. When the signal sounds again, each man takes the nearest woman as a new dance partner and dancing resumes until the signal sounds again. The process is repeated until the crowd is well mixed.

Women go single file clockwise; men go single file counterclockwise

Popcorn

When a Popcorn dance is announced, couples begin dancing to the band's selection of music. After several measures, the leader signals that all dancers on the floor are to change partners, creating an action similar to exploding popcorn. The signal is given at regular intervals, allowing several measures of music between each.

Snowball

To begin a Snowball dance, one couple starts dancing when the music starts. When a signal is given after a few measures of music, the dancers separate and each selects a new partner from among those not dancing. When the signal is given again, after a few more measures, the two couples separate and each dancer finds another new partner among those not dancing. This continues, increasing the number of dancers on the floor each time until it has "snowballed" to include all of the dancers present.

ONE-STEP

Record: Any dance tune
Position: Couple, closed, waist-hand (ballroom) hold
Footwork: Opposite; step directions given for man
Step arrangement: Pattern

The speed at which you do this dance is determined by the tempo of the music and whether you choose to do quick or slow one-steps. Either may be danced for an entire number or they may be danced alternately during the same song.

The one-step can be danced to music played in almost any four-count rhythm, be it swing or polka. Diagrams shown in pattern 2 are for four-count rhythms (see Waltz, slow [p. 120], for three-count rhythm).

STEPS
Pattern 1: quick one-step
1. Man steps left foot forward—count 1.
2. Man steps right foot forward—count 2.
3. Man steps left foot forward—count 3.
4. Man steps right foot forward—count 4.

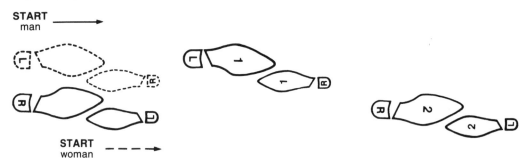

Pattern 1
Step evenly on each beat of music

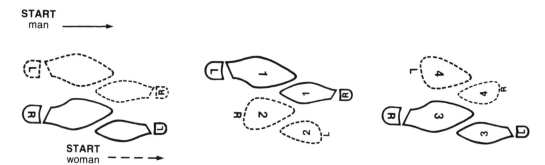

Pattern 2
Step evenly on the first and third beats; touch ball of free foot beside supporting foot on second and fourth beats

Pattern 2: slow one-step

1. Man steps left foot forward—count 1.

2. Man touches ball of right foot beside left foot—count 2 *(variation*: for swing or polka rhythm, flex left knee as ball of foot touches the floor).

3. Man steps right foot forward—count 3.

4. Man touches ball of left foot beside right foot—count 4.

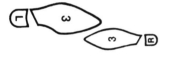

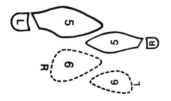

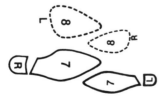

SEVEN-STEP POLKA

The Seven-Step Polka derived from the German tune "Siebenschritt," which means "seven steps."

Record: *Seven-Step Polka*, Bellaire, 5031-B (LH-18868)
Position: Couple, closed, waist-hand (ballroom)
Footwork: Opposite; step directions given for man
Step arrangement: Routine (verse, chorus)

STEPS
Pattern 1, part A: galop (to left)
The sideward steps are taken with a slight up-and-down movement, as if galloping.

1. Man steps left foot sideward to left—count 1(2).

2. Man steps on ball of right foot beside left foot—count 3(4).

3. Man steps left foot sideward to left—count 5(6).

4. Man steps on ball of right foot beside left foot—count 7(8).

5. Man steps left foot sideward to left—count 9.

6. Man steps on ball of right foot beside left foot—count 10.

7. Man steps left foot sideward to left—count 11.

8. Man steps on ball of right foot beside left foot—count 12.

9. Man steps on left foot sideward to left—count 13.

10. Man touches ball of right foot beside left foot—count 14, 15, 16.

Pattern 1, part B: galop (to right)
1. Man steps right foot sideward to right—count 1.

2. Man steps on ball of left foot beside right foot—count 2.

Repeat steps 1 and 2 five times—count 3–12.

3. Man steps right foot sideward to right—count 13.

4. Man touches ball of left foot beside right foot—count 14, 15, 16.

Repeat parts A and B.

Pattern 2: two-steps
Beginning with man's left foot (woman's right) do sixteen turning two-steps (see Two-Step, couple, closed, pp. 113–114).

PUT YOUR LITTLE FOOT (NEW SHOES, VARSOUVIANA)

There are many variations of the basic step for the "Put Your Little Foot" tune. Some are suitable for dancing in couple closed position, others in couple open position, and some may even be danced in spoke-line formation.

A simple two-pattern routine, danced in couple open position using a shoulder (varsouviana) hold, is the one most often seen on Texas dance floors.

Point right toe

Couple, Open Position

Records: Windsor Records, 4615-45; KIK-R, LP 10012

Position: Open, shoulder (varsouviana) hold (this version [without the variation described] may also be danced in spoke-line position using waist holds)

Footwork: Same

Step arrangement: Routine (verse, chorus)

STEPS
Pattern 1, verse: cross-lift (three times), walk, point

1. Cross-lift left foot in front of right ankle—count 1.

2. Step left foot forward—count 2.

3. Step right foot forward beside left foot—count 3.

Repeat steps 1–3 two times—count 4–9.

4. Step left foot forward—count 10.

5. Point right toe diagonally forward to the right—count 11(12).

Repeat steps 1–5, using opposite feet.

Cross-lift right foot over left foot

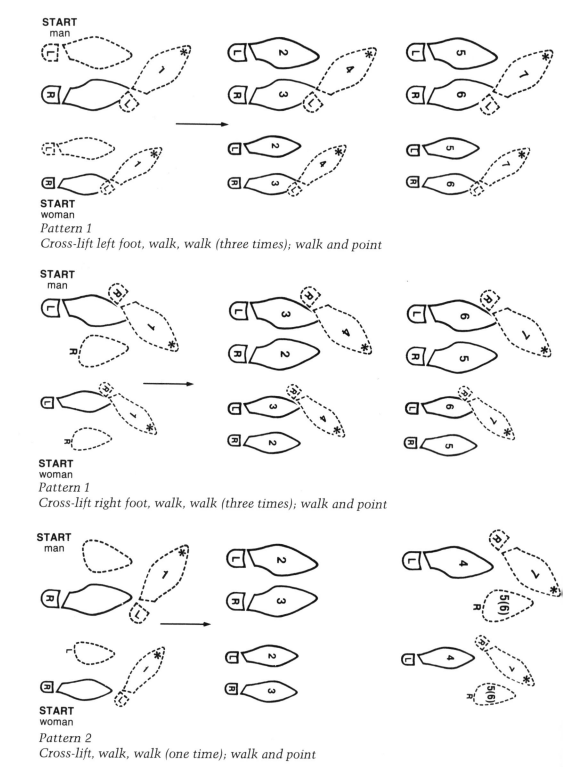

Pattern 1
Cross-lift left foot, walk, walk (three times); walk and point

Pattern 1
Cross-lift right foot, walk, walk (three times); walk and point

Pattern 2
Cross-lift, walk, walk (one time); walk and point

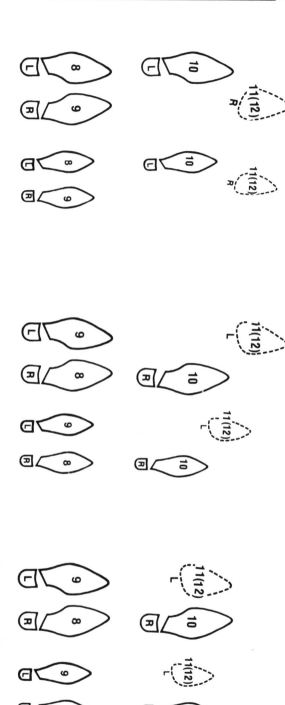

Point right toe (woman on left)

Pattern 2, chorus: cross-lift (one time), walk, point

1. Cross-lift left foot in front of right ankle—count 1.

2. Step left foot forward—count 2.

3. Step right foot forward—count 3.

4. Step left foot forward—count 4.

5. Point right toe diagonally forward to the right—count 5(6) (*variation*: while doing steps 2–4, man moves sideward to the right as woman moves sideward left in front of him to his left side).

Repeat steps 1–5, using opposite feet—count 7–12.

Note: If the variation described above is danced, during the three forward steps, woman crosses sideward left in front of man, returning to his right side.

Repeat pattern 2.

Repeat patterns 1 and 2 to end of music.

Couple Routine, Semi-Closed

In this routine, couples alternate semi-closed V position from side to side. They also alternate between facing LOD and RLOD.

Records: Windsor Records, 4615-45; KIK-R, LP 10012
Position: Semiclosed, waist-hand (ballroom) hold
Footwork: Opposite; step directions given for man
Step arrangement: Routine (verse, chorus)

STEPS
Pattern 1, verse: cross-lift (three times), walk, turn, point

1. Man cross-lifts left foot in front of right ankle—count 1.

2. Man steps left foot forward—count 2.

3. Man steps right foot forward beside left foot—count 3.

Repeat steps 1–3 one time—count 4–6.

4. Man cross-lifts left foot in front of right ankle—count 7.

5. Man steps left foot forward—count 8. (Couple now turn toward each other while turning to face the opposite direction: RLOD. They loosen the waist-hand hold to permit the turn.)

6. Man steps right foot (turned toward partner) forward—count 9.

7. Man steps left foot (heel leading) forward (LOD)—count 10 (couple is now facing reverse direction).

8. Man points right toe forward (RLOD)—count 11(12).

Repeat steps 1–8, using opposite feet in opposite direction.

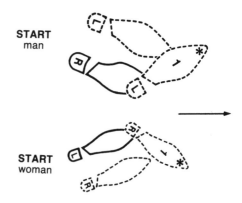

Pattern 1
Cross-lift left foot, walk, walk (three times); turn, and point

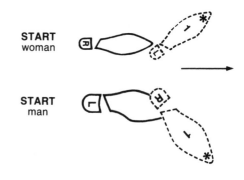

Pattern 1
Cross-lift right foot, walk, walk (three times); turn, and point

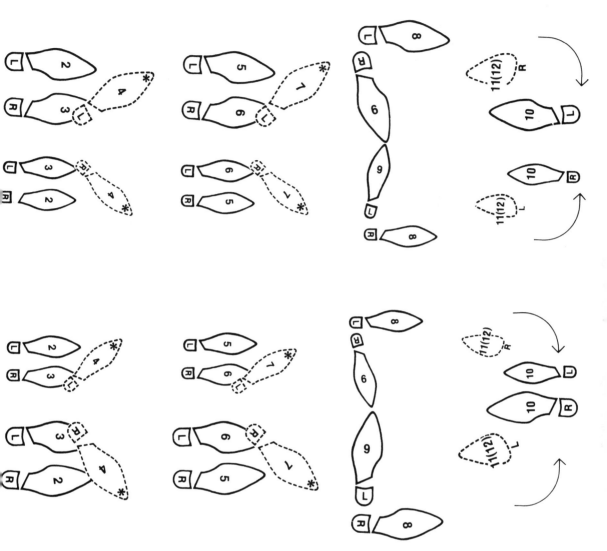

Cross-lift opposite feet across supporting feet

Turn and point in reverse direction

Pattern 2, chorus: cross-lift (one time), walk, turn, point

1. Man cross-lifts left foot in front of right ankle—count 1.

2. Man steps left foot forward—count 2.

3. Man steps right foot (turned toward partner) forward—count 3.

4. Man steps left foot (heel leading) forward—count 4 (couple is now facing reverse direction).

5. Man points right toe forward (RLOD)—count 5(6).

Repeat steps 1–5, using opposite feet in opposite direction.

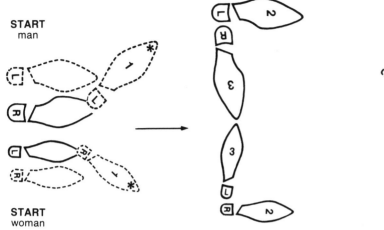

Pattern 2, part A
Cross-lift left foot (one time), turn, and point

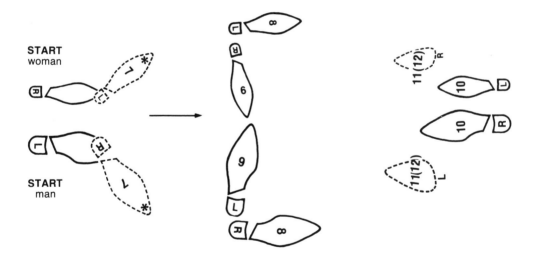

Pattern 2, part B
Cross-lift right foot (one time), turn, and point

TEN PRETTY GIRLS

There are several versions of this dance, but the variations are slight.

Record: *Ten Pretty Girls*, KIK-R, LP-10013
Position: Couple, open, shoulder (varsouviana) hold; spoke-line, waist hold
Footwork: Same
Step arrangement: Routine

STEPS

Pattern 1, part A: toe-touch, grapevine step

1. Cross-touch left toe in front of right foot—count 1(2).
2. Touch left toe diagonally to left—count 3(4).
3. Step left foot sideward right, passing behind right foot (bend knees as legs cross)—count 5.
4. Step right foot sideward right, passing in front of left foot—count 6.

5. Step left foot beside right foot—count 7(8).

Pattern 1, part B: repeat part A, using opposite feet

Pattern 2

Note: When stepping forward, bend supporting knee on second count.

1. Step left foot forward—count 1(2).
2. Step right foot forward—count 3(4).
3. Step left foot forward—count 5(6).
4. Step right foot forward—count 7(8).
5. Extend left foot forward (lean back, keeping body aligned)—count 9(10).
6. Extend left foot backward (lean forward, keeping body aligned)—count 11(12).
7. Step (stamp) left foot in place—count 13.
8. Step (stamp) right foot in place—count 14.
9. Step (stamp) left foot in place—count 15(16).

Repeat patterns 1 and 2, using opposite feet.

Repeat entire sequence to end of music.

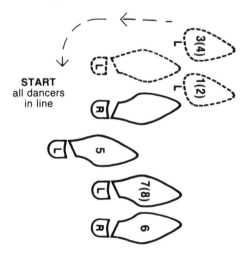

Pattern 1, part A

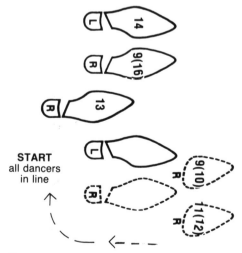

Pattern 1, part B
Toe-touch and grapevine to right; toe-touch and grapevine to left

Cross-touch left toe over right foot

Extend left foot forward, keeping body in alignment while leaning back

Touch left toe diagonally left and forward

Extend left foot backward, keeping body in alignment while leaning forward

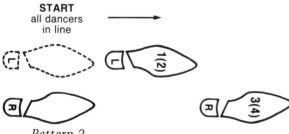

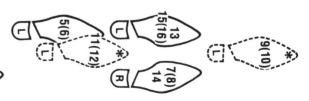

START
all dancers
in line

Pattern 2
Four slow walks, kick forward and backward, stamp three times

TEXAS SHUFFLE STEP

Record: Any four-count music
Position: Couple, waist-hand (ballroom) hold, closed position
Footwork: Opposite; step directions given for man
Step arrangement: Pattern

The Texas Shuffle step was formerly called a foxtrot step and has erroneously been called Texas Two-Step. This error causes confusion because this dance is entirely different from the real two-step as danced in the forward-moving section of Cotton-eyed Joe, Cowboy Polka (Jessie Polka), and other dances.

The shuffle step may be danced to any four-count music and may be danced in forward line of dance direction, sideward, turning, or in place. The shuffle step uses six counts; therefore it takes three four-count measures of music to complete two shuffle steps.

STEPS
Pattern 1: shuffle step, man forward, woman backward

1. Man steps left foot forward—count 1.

2. Man steps right foot forward—count 2.

3. Man steps left foot forward—count 3.

4. Man touches ball of right foot beside left foot—count 4.

5. Man steps right foot forward—count 5.

6. Man touches ball of left foot beside right foot—count 6.

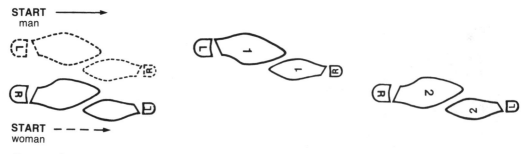

Pattern 1
Quick, quick, slow, slow steps forward for man, backward for woman

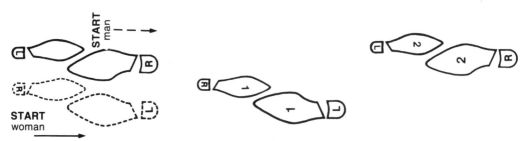

Pattern 2
Quick, quick, slow, slow steps backward for man, forward for woman

Pattern 2: shuffle step, man backward, woman forward

1. Man steps left foot backward—count 1.

2. Man steps right foot backward—count 2.

3. Man steps left foot backward—count 3.

4. Man touches ball of right foot beside left foot—count 4.

5. Man steps right foot backward—count 5.

6. Man touches ball of left foot beside right foot—count 6.

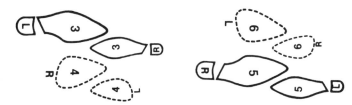

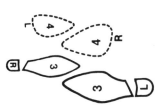
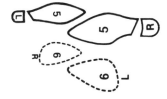

Pattern 3: shuffle-step turn

1. Man steps left foot forward, turning one-quarter left—count 1.

2. Man steps right foot backward, turning one-quarter left—count 2.

3. Man steps left foot forward, turning one-quarter left—count 3.

4. Man touches ball of right foot beside left foot—count 4.

5. Man steps right foot backward, turning one-quarter left—count 5.

6. Man touches ball of left foot beside right foot—count 6.

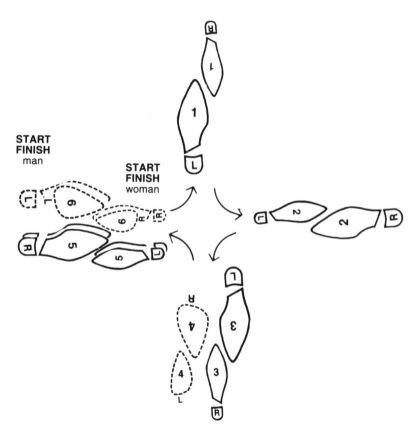

Pattern 3
Shuffle-step left turn

TWO-STEP, POLKA
TWO- STEP

The two-step and polka two-step may be danced forward, backward, sideward, or turning; in a spoke-line, individually, or in closed position. To change the standard two-step to a "Texas style" polka two-step, dancers should hop on the fourth counts. Directions for making this change are shown in parentheses. Some people do the two-step to waltz music and think they are waltzing.

Spoke-line, Couple, Open

Record: Any four-count dance music for the two-step; any polka dance music for the polka two-step
Position: Spoke-line, waist hold; couple, open, shoulder (varsouviana) hold
Footwork: Same
Step arrangement: Pattern

STEPS
Pattern 1: forward two-steps
   1. Step left foot forward—count 1.
   2. Step right foot forward beside left foot—count 2.
   3. Step left foot forward—count 3(4). (Polka two-step: on count 4, hop on left foot.)
   4. Step right foot forward—count 5.
   5. Step left foot forward beside right foot—count 6.
   6. Step right foot forward—count 7(8). (Polka two-step: on count 8, hop on right foot.)

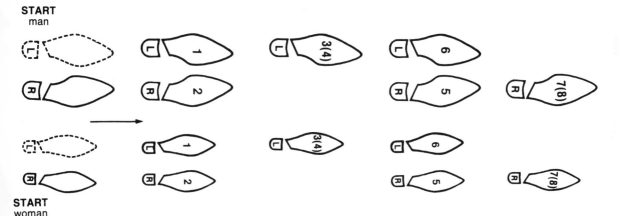

START
man

START
woman

Pattern 1
Two-step forward

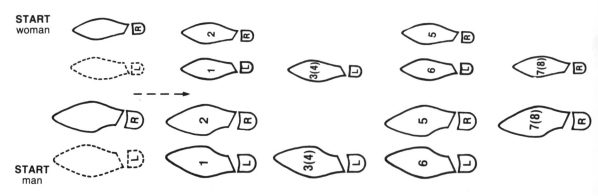

Pattern 2
Two-step backward

Pattern 2: backward two-steps
1. Step left foot backward—count 1.
2. Step right foot backward beside left foot—count 2.
3. Step left foot backward—count 3(4).
(Polka two-step: on count 4, hop on left foot.)

4. Step right foot backward—count 5.
5. Step left foot backward beside right foot—count 6.
6. Step right foot backward—count 7(8).
(Polka two-step: on count 8, hop on right foot.)

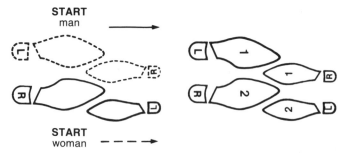

Pattern 1, Couple, closed
Two-step forward for man, backward for woman

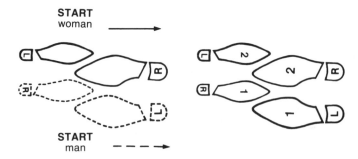

Pattern 2, Couple, closed
Two-step backward for man, forward for woman

Couple, Closed

Record: Same as for spoke-line, couple, open
Position: Couple, closed, waist-hand (ballroom) hold
Footwork: Opposite; step directions given for man
Step arrangement: Pattern

Pattern 1: couple, closed, two-step (or polka two-step)

1. Man steps left foot forward—count 1.

2. Man steps right foot forward beside left foot—count 2.

3. Man steps left foot forward—count 3(4).

(Polka two-step: on count 4, man hops on left foot.)

4. Man steps right foot forward—count 5.

5. Man steps left foot forward beside right foot—count 6.

6. Man steps right foot forward—count 7(8).

(Polka two-step: on count 8, man hops on right foot.)

Pattern 2: couple, closed, two-step backward

1. Man steps left foot backward—count 1.

2. Man steps right foot backward beside left foot—count 2.

3. Man steps left foot backward—count 3(4).

(Polka two-step: on count 4, man hops on left foot.)

4. Man steps right foot backward—count 5.

5. Man steps left foot backward beside right foot—count 6.

6. Man steps right foot backward—count 7(8).

(Polka two-step: on count 8, man hops on right foot.)

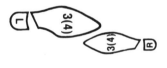

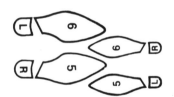

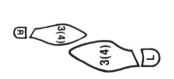

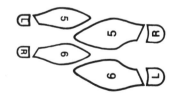

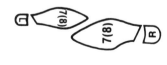

Beginning two-step position

Man steps left foot forward; woman steps right foot backward

Pattern 3: two-step box

1. Man steps left foot sideward left—count 1.

2. Man steps right foot left beside left—count 2.

3. Man steps left foot forward—count 3(4).

(Polka two-step: on count 4, man hops on left foot.)

4. Man steps right foot sideward to right—count 5.

5. Man steps left foot sideward to right beside right—count 6.

6. Man steps right foot backward—count 7(8).

(Polka two-step: on count 8, man hops on right foot.)

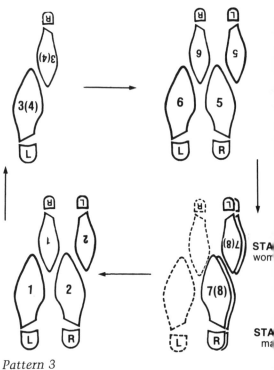

Pattern 3
Two-step box

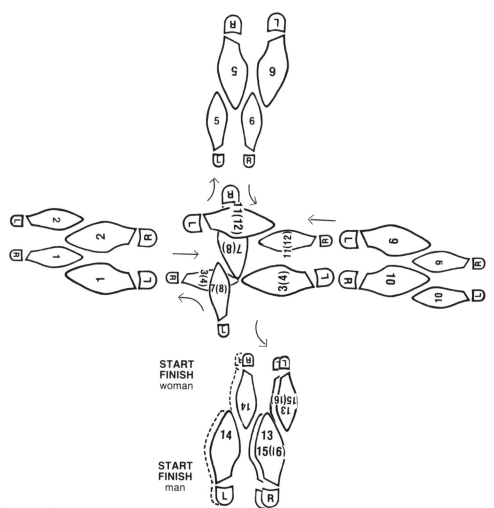

Pattern 4
Two-step left turn

Pattern 4: two-step left turn

Single-count steps, such as 1 and 2, are taken while turning to four sides of a square formation; double-count steps, such as 3(4), are taken in the center of the square.

1. Man steps left foot forward, one-quarter turn to left—count 1.

2. Man steps right foot beside left—count 2.

3. Man steps left foot backward—count 3(4).

(Polka two-step: on count 4, man hops on left foot.)

4. Man steps right foot backward, one-quarter turn to left—count 5.

5. Man steps left foot backward beside right foot—count 6.

6. Man steps right foot forward—count 7(8).

(Polka two-step: on count 8, man hops on right foot.)

7. Man steps left foot forward, one-quarter turn to left—count 9.

Man steps right foot forward beside his left foot; woman steps left foot backward beside her right foot

Man steps left foot forward; woman steps right foot backward to complete one two-step

8. Man steps right foot forward beside left foot—count 10.

9. Man steps left foot backward—count 11(12).

(Polka two-step: on count 12, man hops on left foot.)

10. Man steps right foot backward, one-quarter turn to left (returning to original place)—count 13.

11. Man steps left foot backward beside right foot—count 14.

12. Man steps right foot in place—count 15(16).

(Polka two-step: on count 16, man hops on right foot.)

Pattern 5: two-step right turn

Repeat pattern 4 in reverse direction, using opposite feet, and beginning with right foot forward, one-quarter turn to the right.

WALTZ ACROSS TEXAS, SPOKE-LINE WALTZ

The following spoke-line waltz routine is a 1980 Betty Casey original. Although it may be danced to any waltz dance music, it goes especially well with "Waltz across Texas," an old favorite written by a renowned Texas country-western musician, Ernest Tubb. It may also be danced by a couple in open position, using a shoulder (varsouviana) hold.

Records: Any waltz dance music; for example, *Waltz across Texas*, SunRa, SRR-0002-B; Crescendo GNPS 2139
Position: Spoke-line, waist hold; couple, open, shoulder (varsouviana) hold
Footwork: Same
Step arrangement: Routine (verse, chorus)

Spoke-line or Couple Waltz

STEPS

Pattern 1, part A, verse: waltz-steps, forward
   1. Step left foot forward—count 1.
   2. Step right foot forward—count 2.
   3. Step left foot forward beside right foot—count 3.
   4. Step right foot forward—count 4.
   5. Step left foot forward—count 5.
   6. Step right foot forward beside left foot—count 6.
   Repeat steps 1–6—count 7–12.

START
all dancers
in line

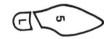

Pattern 1, part A
Two waltz-steps forward

Pattern 1, part B, verse: waltz dip, forward waltz (in place)

 1. Step left foot backward—count 1.

 2. Extend raised right foot forward—count 2(3).

 3. Step right foot forward—count 4.

 4. Step left foot forward beside right foot—count 5.

 5. Step right foot beside left foot—count 6.

 Repeat steps 1–5.

 Repeat parts A and B.

Pattern 2, part A, chorus: waltz cross-step

 1. Cross-step left foot forward in front of right foot—count 1.

 2. Step right foot forward—count 2.

 3. Step left foot forward beside right foot—count 3.

 4. Cross-step right foot forward in front of left foot—count 4.

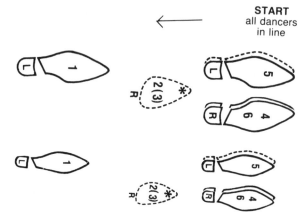

Pattern 1, part B
Dip backward, forward waltz (in place)

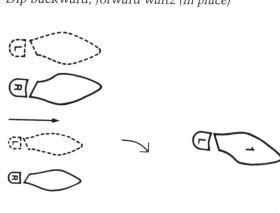

Pattern 2, part A
Line waltz cross-step

5. Step left foot forward—count 5.

6. Step right foot forward beside left foot—count 6.

Repeat steps 1–6.

Pattern 2, part B, chorus: waltz dip, forward waltz (in place)

1. Repeat pattern 2, part B—count 1–12.

Repeat entire sequence to end of music.

Dip backward on left foot

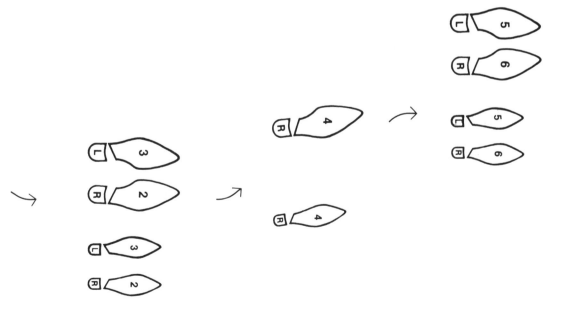

WALTZ, COUPLE

A two-step ends with feet spread wide,
A waltz step leaves feet side-by-side.

Record: Any waltz dance music
Position: Couple, closed, semiclosed,
waist-hand (ballroom) hold
Footwork: Opposite; step directions
given for man
Step arrangement: Pattern

Waltzes may be danced in spoke-line
formations and in couple positions.
Eight couple waltz patterns are described
here. Line waltz-patterns, which may
also be danced to any waltz dance music,
are described in the Waltz across Texas
section.

Some people do the two-step to waltz
music because they think they are waltzing. This may be because each requires
the same number of steps, although a
waltz calls for a three-count beat and the
two-step is done to a four-count beat.
This rhyme defines the difference:

STEPS
Pattern 1: couple, forward waltz-step
1. Man steps left foot forward—
count 1.
2. Man steps right foot forward—
count 2.
3. Man steps left foot forward beside
right foot—count 3.
4. Man steps right foot forward—
count 4.
5. Man steps left foot forward—
count 5.

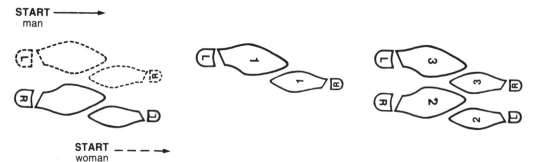

Pattern 1
Waltz forward for man, backward for woman

Pattern 2
Waltz backward for man, forward for woman

6. Man steps right foot forward beside left foot—count 6.

Pattern 2: couple, backward waltz-step

1. Man steps left foot backward—count 1.

2. Man steps right foot backward—count 2.

3. Man steps left foot backward beside right foot—count 3.

4. Man steps right foot backward—count 4.

5. Man steps left foot backward—count 5.

6. Man steps right foot backward beside left foot—count 6.

Pattern 3: couple, left-turn waltz-step

1. Man steps left foot forward and one-quarter turn to left—count 1.

2. Man backs right foot forward LOD (with foot toed-in so heel is leading) one-

quarter turn to left to face backward in RLOD—count 2.

3. Man backs left foot to place beside right foot—count 3.

Note: Dancers should now be facing opposite, RLOD, from beginning direction.

4. Man backs right foot forward LOD, heel leading, one-quarter turn to left—count 4.

5. Man steps left foot forward and one-quarter turn to left—count 5.

6. Man steps right foot one-quarter turn to left beside right foot—count 6.

Note: Dancers should now be facing in original direction.

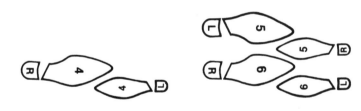

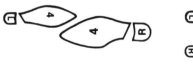

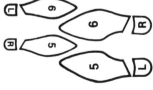

Pattern 4: couple, right-turn waltz-step

Note: This pattern begins when the man's right (and woman's left) foot is free, as shown in pattern 1, step 3.

1. Man steps right foot forward and one-quarter turn to right—count 1.

2. Man backs left foot forward LOD (with foot toed-in so heel is leading) one-quarter turn to right to face backward in RLOD—count 2.

3. Man backs right foot to place beside left foot—count 3.

Note: Dancers should now be facing opposite, RLOD, from beginning direction.

4. Man backs left foot forward LOD, heel leading, one-quarter turn to right—count 4.

5. Man steps right foot forward and one-quarter turn to right—count 5.

6. Man steps left foot beside right foot—count 6.

Note: Dancers should now be facing in original direction.

Pattern 5: couple, closed, slow waltz-step

1. Man steps left foot forward—count 1.

2. Man touches ball of right foot beside left foot—count 2(3).

3. Man steps right foot forward—count 4.

4. Man touches ball of left foot beside right foot—count 5(6).

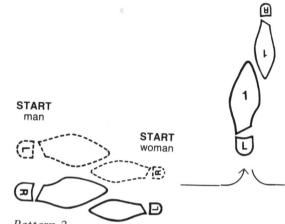

Pattern 3
Waltz turn: left for man, right for woman

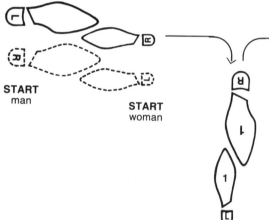

Pattern 4
Waltz turn: right for man, left for woman

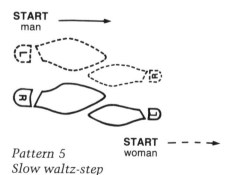

Pattern 5
Slow waltz-step

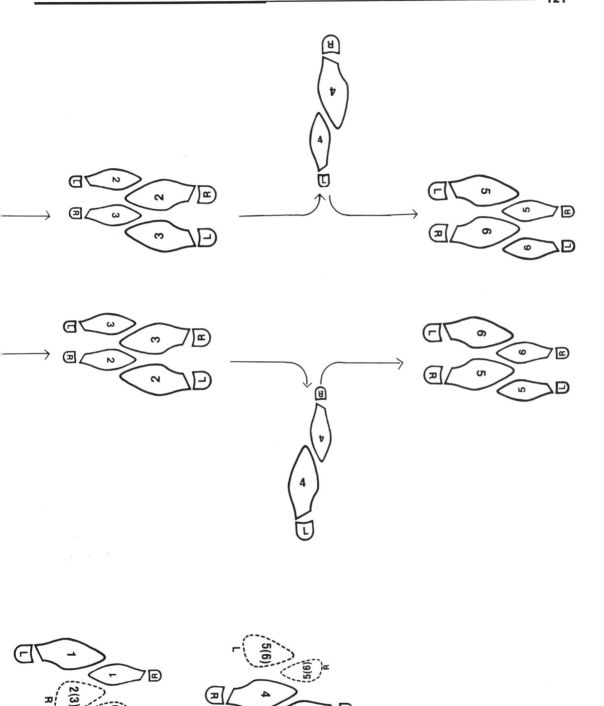

Beginning waltz position

Man steps left foot forward; woman steps right foot backward

Pattern 6: couple, closed, waltz box

1. Man steps left foot forward—count 1.

2. Man steps right foot sideward to right—count 2.

3. Man steps left foot sideward right beside right foot—count 3.

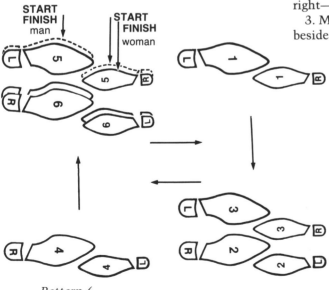

Pattern 6
Waltz box for couple

Man steps right foot forward; woman steps left foot backward

Man steps left foot forward beside right; woman steps right foot backward beside left

4. Man steps right foot backward—count 4.

5. Man steps left foot sideward to left (back to original place)—count 5.

6. Man steps right foot sideward left beside left foot—count 6.

Pattern 7: couple, closed, waltz dip

Note: During the dip, the dancers should lean slightly (man backward, woman forward), so their bodies are in alignment with their extended legs.

1. Man steps left foot backward and leans back slightly. Woman simultaneously steps right foot forward and leans slightly forward—count 1.

2. Man lifts extended right leg forward (toe extended in a point) a few inches from the floor. Woman lifts extended left leg backward (toe extended in a point) just above and in alignment with the man's leg—count 2(3).

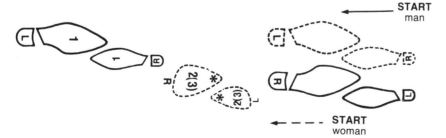

Pattern 7
Waltz dip for couple

Pattern 8, part A: couple, closed, waist-hand (ballroom) hold, waltz cross-step

Note: The waist-hand hold must be loosened and adjusted to allow for steps to be taken in between partners.

1. Man steps left foot diagonally with toe leading across in front of his right foot, between him and his partner. Woman steps right foot diagonally with heel leading, across in back of her left foot—count 1.

2. Man steps right foot sideward to right and forward. Woman steps left foot sideward to left and backward—count 2.

3. Man steps left foot beside his right foot. Woman steps right foot beside her left foot—count 3.

Pattern 8, part B

4. Man steps right foot, diagonally with toe leading, across in front of his left foot, between him and his partner. Woman steps left foot diagonally with heel leading, across in back of her right foot—count 4.

5. Man steps left foot sideward to left and forward. Woman steps right foot sideward right and backward—count 2.

6. Man steps right foot beside his left foot. Woman steps left foot beside her right foot—count 6.

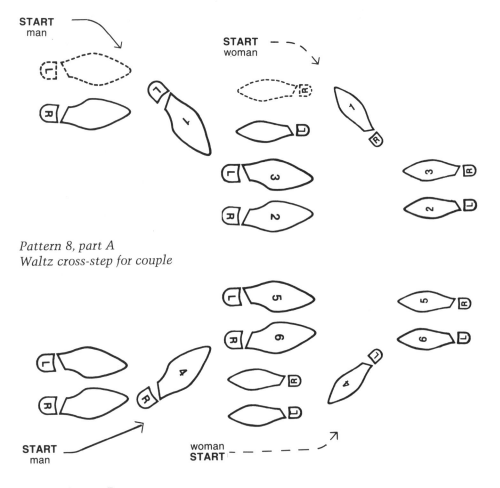

Pattern 8, part A
Waltz cross-step for couple

Pattern 8, part B
Waltz cross-step for couple

WESTERN SCHOTTISCHE

The Western Schottische may be danced either by couples or in spoke-lines.

Spoke-line

Records: MacGregor, 5003-A-45; KIK-R, LP 10012
Position: Spoke-line, waist hold
Footwork: Same
Step arrangement: Routine (verse, chorus)

STEPS

Pattern 1, part A, verse: grapevine left, step-hop

1. Step left foot sideward to left—count 1.

2. Step right foot sideward to left, passing in back of and to left side of left foot (bend knees as legs cross)—count 2.

3. Step left foot sideward to left, passing in front of and to left side of right foot—count 3.

4. Hop on left foot and raise right foot by bending knee—count 4.

Pattern 1, part B, verse: grapevine right, step-hop

1. Step right foot sideward to right—count 5.

2. Step left foot sideward to right, passing in back of and to right side of right foot (bend knees as legs cross)—count 6.

3. Step right foot sideward to right, passing in front of and to right side of left foot—count 7.

4. Hop on right foot and raise left foot by bending knee—count 8.

Variation: The grapevine steps may be replaced with three forward running steps.

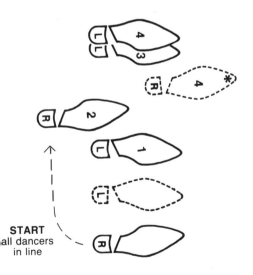

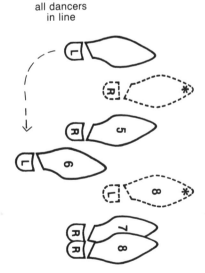

Pattern 1, part A   Part B

Grapevine left, step-hop; grapevine right, step-hop

Cross-step left across right

Step-hop

Pattern 2, chorus: step-hop forward

When hopping on one foot, raise other foot by bending knee.

1. Step left foot forward—count 9.

2. Hop on left while raising right foot—count 10.

3. Step right foot forward—count 11.

4. Hop on right while raising left foot—count 12.

Repeat steps 1–4—count 13–16.

Repeat patterns 1 and 2 to end of music.

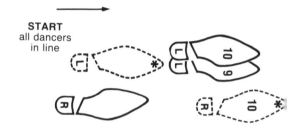

Pattern 2
Step-hop forward

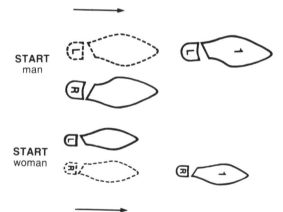

Pattern 1
Couple run, step-hop

Couple

Records: Same as spoke-line
Position: Couple, semiclosed; waist-
    hand (ballroom) hold
Footwork: Opposite; step directions
    given for man
Step arrangement: Routine (verse,
    chorus)

Pattern 1, verse: run, step-hop
    Forward steps are taken as if running
lightly. When hopping on one foot, raise
other foot by bending knee.
    1. Man steps left foot forward—
count 1.
    2. Man steps right foot forward—
count 2.

3. Man steps left foot forward—
count 3.
    4. Man hops on left foot while raising
right foot—count 4.
    5. Man steps right foot forward—
count 5.
    6. Man steps left foot forward—
count 6.
    7. Man steps right foot forward—
count 7.
    8. Man hops on right foot while rais-
ing left foot—count 8.

*Pattern 2, chorus: rocking forward and
backward*
    When rocking (leaning) forward and
backward, bend weight-bearing knee on
second beat (i.e., lean—count 1, bend—
count 2).

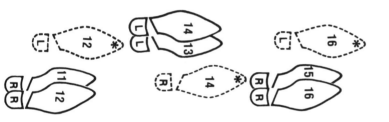

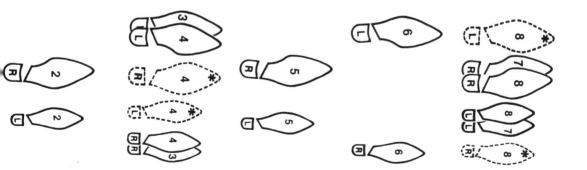

Step-hop, outside foot

Step-hop, inside foot

1. Man leans forward on left foot—count 1(2).

2. Man leans backward on right foot—count 3(4).

3. Man leans forward on left foot—count 5(6).

4. Man leans backward on right foot—count 7(8).

Variations: (1) The couple may turn in a full circle while doing steps 1–4 by turning one-quarter on each step; (2) the couple may continue moving forward on steps 1–4 by alternating step-hops beginning with the man's left foot; (3) step-hop forward (as in spoke-line routine, pattern 2) may be substituted for the leaning forward and knee bending; (4) the Horse and Buggy Schottische is danced by two couples holding hands in tandem formation—one couple in front of the other. For pattern 1, verse, they do the same step described for a couple. For pattern 2, chorus, each dancer does four step-hops. While doing this, the lead couple only (the horses) releases hands, separates, and fans out at each side to circle around to become the following couple (the buggy).

Step-flex knee, outside foot

WESTERN SWING

Described here are the basic swing step and the turn-under, both popular on Texas dance floors.

Record: Any swing dance music
Position: Alternating closed, semiclosed, waist-hand (ballroom) hold; facing, one-hand hold
Footwork: Opposite; step directions given for man, except as noted
Step arrangement: Pattern

STEPS
It takes three measures of four-count music to complete two basic swing steps. Synchronized push-and-pull hand movements and rhythmic flexing of the knees are basic features of this dance.

Pattern 1: basic swing step, closed position

1. Man steps left foot sideward to left—count 1.
2. Man touches ball of right foot be-side left foot, at same time flexing left knee—count 2.
3. Man steps right foot sideward to right—count 3.
4. Man touches ball of left foot beside right foot, at same time flexing right knee—count 4.

Note: For next step, partners push gently against each other's hands (man's left, woman's right) to open into the V of semiclosed position.

5. Man steps left foot, heel leading, behind and at right angle to his right foot, and raises his right foot slightly—count 5.

Note: Partners quickly pull each other back to closed position during next step.

6. Man steps right foot back in starting position—count 6.

Repeat steps 1–6 as many times as desired.

Pattern 2, part A: turn-under step

The man and woman follow entirely different patterns and positions in the turn-under while using the same count. Each pattern is described separately, but count number is noted only once. The woman drops her left arm from man's shoulder and he gently pushes her waist with his right hand to help her start turning forward and to the right under the joined man's left and woman's right hands. The hands swivel in a loose grasp as she goes under them.

1. *Man* steps left foot backward at right angle behind his right foot. Simultaneously, *woman* steps to right—count 1.
2. *Man* touches ball of right foot parallel to and beside his left foot, at same time flexing left knee. Simultaneously, *woman* touches ball of left foot parallel to and beside her right, at same time flexing her right knee—count 2.
3. *Man* steps right foot slightly backward. Simultaneously, *woman* turns left foot and with heel leading, steps outward—count 3.

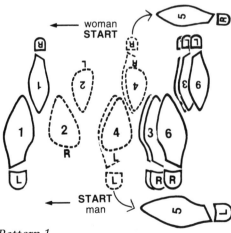

Pattern 1
Basic swing step

4. *Man* touches ball of left foot beside his right foot, at same time flexing his right knee. Simultaneously, *woman* touches ball of right foot parallel to and beside her left foot, at same time flexing her left knee—count 4.

5. *Man* steps left foot slightly backward. *Woman* steps right foot slightly backward—count 5.

Note: Dancers should now be turned one-quarter to man's left from starting position and be about two feet apart with joined hands outstretched. Both lean shoulders back and quickly stretch away, then pull each other forward.

6. *Man* steps right foot forward. *Woman* steps left foot forward—count 6.

Pattern 2, part B: turn-under step

Note: In returning to starting closed position, woman backs under joined hands, turning to the left.

1. *Man* steps left foot forward. *Woman* steps right foot forward at a right angle in front of left foot—count 7.

2. *Man* touches ball of right foot beside his left foot, at same time flexing left knee. *Woman* touches ball of left foot parallel to and beside her right foot,

at same time flexing her right knee—count 8.

3. *Man* steps right foot forward. *Woman* steps left foot forward turned left at right angle to her right foot—count 9.

4. *Man* touches ball of left foot beside his right foot, at same time flexing his right knee. *Woman* touches ball of right foot parallel to and beside left foot, at same time flexing left knee—count 10.

Note: In next step, dancers step backward from each other, lean shoulders back, and give a quick, gentle stretch-pull against each other.

5. *Man* steps left foot backward at right angle to his right foot. *Woman* steps right foot backward at right angle to her left foot—count 11.

Dancers pull forward into starting positions.

6. *Man* steps right foot forward into starting position. *Woman* steps left foot forward into starting position.

Repeat parts A and B as many times as desired.

Patterns 1 and 2 may be danced in any combination.

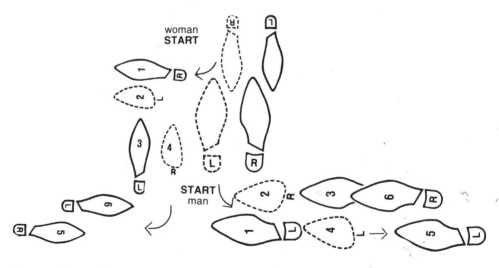

Pattern 2, part A
Turn-under step

Turn-under

Stretch-pull

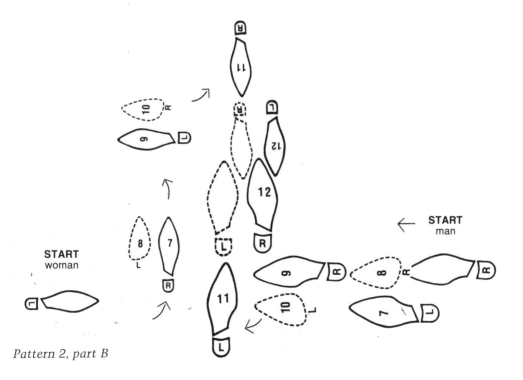

Pattern 2, part B

Bibliography

American Square Dancing through the Years, 1776–1976. Anaheim, Cal.: National Square Dance Convention, 1976.

Anderson, W. D. "Kappa Chi Fraternity." File AF U 4500 (2), Austin, Texas, Public Library, History Center, n.d.

Angle, Joe. "Fiddlers and Festivals: A Texas Tradition." In *Some Still Do: Essays on Texas Customs*, pp. 59–71. Texas Folklore Society, vol. 39. Austin: Encino Press, 1975.

Arnold, Charles August. "The Folk-Lore, Manners, and Customs of the Mexicans in San Antonio, Texas." University of Texas, August 1928.

"Artists/Entertainers." In *Who's Who in Country and Western Music*. Culver City, Cal.: Black Stallion Press, 1981.

Ashby, Lynn. "Live, It's Saturday Night at Crider's." *Houston Post*, July 15, 1979.

Ball, Aimee Lee. "The Adventures of an Urban Cowgirl." *Redbook*. January 1981.

Barnes, Charles Merritt. *Combats and Conquests of Immortal Heroes*. San Antonio: Guessaz & Ferlet Co., 1910.

Barney, Bill. *The Bright Side of Country Life*. Dallas: Farmers' Publishing Co., 1906.

Bertram, Jack. "Martinez 'Father of Conjunto'!" *Kerrville Daily Times*, August 17, 1983.

Boatright, Mody C., Wilson M. Hudson, and Allen Maxwell, eds. *Texas Folk and Folklore*. Folklore Society, no. 26. Dallas: Southern Methodist University Press, 1954.

Bode, Elroy. "Crider's." In *Elroy Bode's Sketchbook II*, pp. 1–5. El Paso: Texas Western Press, 1972.

Brandenberg, Nancy Fly. "Great Country Dance Halls." *Magazine of San Antonio*. October 1979.

Burchett, Chet. "Texas Remains Unique Experience." *Waco Tribune-Herald*, June 11, 1980.

Bushick, Frank H. *Glamorous Days*. San Antonio: Naylor Co., 1934.

Carroll, Elder B. H. *Modern Social Dance, a Sermon*. Dallas: Texas Baptist Publishing House, 1877.

Casey, Betty. *The Complete Book of Square Dancing (and Round Dancing)*. Garden City, N.Y.: Doubleday & Co., 1981.

———. *International Folk Dancing, U.S.A.* Garden City, N.Y.: Doubleday & Co., 1976.

———. "Square Dancing, USA." *Viltis* (Denver). June–August 1979.

Centennial Committee, Harper County. *Here's Harper, 1863–1963*. Fredericksburg, Tex.: Radio Post, 1963.

Chittenden, William Lawrence. *Ranch Verses*. New York: G. P. Putnam's Sons, 1893.

Clarke, Mary Whatley. "The Founding of the Matador." *Cattleman*. October 1956.

———. *The Swenson Saga and the SMS Ranches*. Austin: Jenkins Publishing Co., 1976.

Cleveland, C. H., Jr. *Dancing at Home and Abroad*. Boston: Oliver Ditson and Co., 1878.

"Constitution and By-Laws of the German Club of Kerr County." Kerrville, Tex., 1934.

Craddock, John R. "The Cowboy Dance." In *Texas Folk and Folklore*, edited by Mody C. Boatright, Wilson M. Hudson, and Allen Maxwell, pp. 183–189. Dallas: Southern Methodist University Press, 1954.

Crawford, Ann Fears, and Crystal Sasse Ragsdale. *Women in Texas*. Burnet, Tex.: Eakin Press, 1982.

Czompo, Ann I. "Disco Dancing." *JOPER* (Reston, Va.). April 1980.

Dale, Edward Everett. *The Cross Timbers: Memories of a North Texas Boyhood*. Austin: University of Texas Press, 1966.

Dobie, J. Frank, Mody C. Boatright, and Harry H. Ransom. *Texian Stomping Grounds*. Austin: Texas Folk-Lore Society, 1941.

Duke, Mrs. R. L. "A Christmas Gift from Monkeyface." *Cattleman*. December 1953.

Duke, Cordia Sloan, and Joe B. Frantz. *6,000 Miles of Fence: Life on the XIT Ranch of Texas*. Austin: University of Texas Press, 1961.

Ellis, Anna. "Social Life in Old Texas Days Alive with Thrills—Gayety, Too." *San Antonio Express*, October 13, 1934.

Farrell, Mary D., and Elizabeth Silverthorne. *First Ladies of Texas*. Belton, Tex.: Stillhouse Hollow Publishers, 1976.

Fenley, Florence. *Oldtimers: Their Own Stories*. Uvalde, Tex.: Hornsby Press, 1929.

———. *Oldtimers of Southwest Texas*. Uvalde, Tex.: Hornsby Press, 1957.

Flach, Vera. *A Yankee in German-America*. San Antonio: Naylor Co., 1973.

Fodor's Texas. New York: Fodor's Travel Guides, 1983.

"The Folk Dance of America—What Does It Mean." *Square Dancing*. July 1982.

Frantz, Joe B., Robert K. Holz, Mildred P. Mayhall, and Sam W. Newman. *Texas and Its History*. 2d ed. Dallas: Pepper Jones Martinez, Publishers, 1978.

Froneberger, Jean. "Remembering Crider Comforts." *Texas Observer*, September 16, 1983.

Gard, Wayne. *Rawhide Texas*. Norman: University of Oklahoma Press, 1965.

"Gilley's Remains Honky-tonk King." *San Antonio Sunday Express-News*, August 14, 1983.

Gottschalk, Earl C., Jr. "New Nightclubs Are Different: The Bull Throws the People." *Wall Street Journal*, October 9, 1980.

Gray, Frank S. *Pioneering in Southwest Texas*. Austin: Steck Co., 1949.

Green, Bill. *The Dancing Was Lively*. San Angelo, Tex.: Fort Concho Sketches Publishing Co., 1974.

Haley, Michael. "The Western Wave." *Delta Sky*. 1980.

Harper, Minnie Timms. "Memorable Dance at Matador Ranch in 1895." *Fort Worth Star-Telegram*, March 15, 1936.

———, and George Dewey. *Old Ranches*. Dallas: Dealey and Lowe, 1936.

Harris, Dilue Rose. *The Quarterly of the Texas State Historical Association* 4, no. 2 (October 1900): 85–127; 4, no. 3 (January 1901): 155–189; 7, no. 3 (January 1904): 214–222.

Harris, Jane A., Anne Pittman, and Marlys S. Waller. *Dance a While*. Minneapolis: Burgess Publishing Co., 1950.

Harris, Sallie B. *Cowmen and Ladies*. Canyon, Tex.: Staked Plains Press, 1981.

Hart, Katherine. "Austin's Social Season Used to Be a Humdinger." *Austin American-Statesman*, January 8, 1972.

Hendrix, John M. "Cowboys Had Fun in the 'Gay 90s.'" *Cattleman*. March 1935.

———. *If I Can Do It Horseback*. Austin: University of Texas Press, 1964.

Hines, John. "Sons of the Pioneers Open Up Lots of Happy Trails." *San Antonio Express News*, November 23, 1980.

Hogan, William Ransom. "Amusements in the Republic of Texas." *Journal of Southern History* 5, nos. 3 & 4 (November 1937): 397–341.

———. *The Texas Republic*. 1946. Reprint. Austin: University of Texas Press, 1969.

Holck, Manfred. "A Century of Singing, 'Das Deutsche Lied,' Austin Saenger-runde, 1879–1979." 1979.

Holden, William Curry. *Alkali Trails*. Dallas: Southwest Press, 1930.

Holland, W. B. *The Dance Indicted, a Sermon*. Brownwood, Tex.: Central Messenger Print, n.d.

"In the Whirl of Society." *Austin Tribune*, October 27, 1901.

Isbell, Branch. "Ranch Dances Recalled." *Cattleman*. October 1926.

James, Vinton Lee. *Frontier and Pioneer Recollections of Early Days in San Antonio and West Texas*. San Antonio: Artes Graficas, 1938.

Jenkins, John Holland, III, ed. *Recollections of Early Texas*. Austin: University of Texas Press, 1958.

Jensen, Mary Bee and Clayne R. *Folk Dancing*. Provo: Brigham Young University Press, 1973.

Lake, Mary Daggett. *Pioneer Christmas Customs of Tarrant County*. Texas Folk-Lore Society, no. 5. Austin, 1926.

"A Large German." *Austin Daily Statesman*, May 4, 1889.

Lee, James Ward. "The Glamour of the Gay Night Life—The Classic Honky Tonk." In *T for Texas*. Nacogdoches: Texas Folklore Society, 1982.

Leisner, Tony. *The Official Guide to Country Dance Steps*. Secaucus, N.J.: Chartwell Books, 1980.

Livingston, Peter. *The Complete Book of Country Swing and Western Dance and a Bit about Cowboys*. New York: Doubleday & Co., 1981.

Lomax, John A., and Alan Lomax. *American Ballads and Folk Songs*. New York: Macmillan Co., 1934.

McKay, S. S. *Social Conditions in Texas in the Eighteen Seventies*. Abilene: West Texas Historical Association, 1938.

Malone, Bill C. *Country Music, U.S.A.* American Folklore Society Memoir Series, vol. 54. Austin: University of Texas Press, 1968.

Marks, Joseph E., III. "The Mathers on Dancing." *Dance Horizons*. 1975.

Maverick, Mary A. *Memoirs of Mary A. Maverick*. San Antonio: Alamo Printing Co., 1921.

"The Military Ball." *Austin Daily Statesman*, July 17, 1894.

Munday Historical Society. *"My Home Town": A History of Munday, Texas*. Archer City, Tex.: McCrain Publishing Co., 1981.

Murray, Arthur. *How to Become a Good Dancer*. New York: Simon & Schuster, 1959.

Nettel, Reginald. *Folk-Dancing*. London: Taylor Garnett Evans and Co., 1962.

Neu, Carol. "After Exams, Grandma Danced All Night." File AF U 4500 (2), Austin, Texas, Public Library, History Center, n.d.

Newcomb, Pearson. *The Alamo City*. San Antonio: Standard Printing Company Press, 1926.

Oehler, Herbert E. *Hill Country Boy*. Kerrville, Tex.: Herring Printing Co. for Hill Country Preservation Society, 1980.

Penn, W. E. *There Is No Harm in Dancing*. St. Louis: Lewis E. Kline, Publisher and Bookseller. 1884.

Pinkard, Tommie. "A Lively Sworray." *Texas Highways*. December 1979.

Porterfield, Bill. *The Greatest Honky Tonks in Texas*. Dallas: Taylor Publishing Co., 1983.

Pugh, Donald Wagner. "Music in Frontier Houston, 1836–1876." Master's thesis, University of Texas, 1970.

Ransleben, Guido E. *A Hundred Years of Comfort in Texas*. 1954. Reprint. San Antonio: Naylor Co., 1974.

"San Antonio German Club History." San Antonio, 1983. Courtesy Manson A. Olson, Jr., and Richard P. Corrigan.

Sappington, Joe. "The Old Square Dance." *Frontier Times* (Bandera, Tex.). July 1926.

Saunders, George W., ed. *The Trail Drivers of Texas*. Vol. 2. Old Time Trail

Drivers' Association, 1923–1925.

Sawyer, Eve Lynn. "German Club Debutantes to Take Bows." *San Antonio Sunday Express-News*. October 1983.

Schmitz, Joseph William, S.M. *Thus They Lived*. San Antonio: Naylor Co., 1936.

Scott, Roy S. "Up the Trail with the Texan and His Herd Went the Cowboy Ballads." *Cattleman*. August 1929.

Shaw, Lloyd. *Cowboy Dances: A Collection of Western Square Dances*. Caldwell, Idaho: Caxton Printers, 1948.

———. *The Round Dance Book: A Century of Waltzing*. Caldwell, Idaho: Caxton Printers, 1948.

Simpson, Col. Harold B. *Frontier Forts of Texas*. Waco: Texian Press, 1966.

Smithsonian Collection of Classic Country Music, selected and annotated by Bill C. Malone. Washington, D.C., 1981.

Smithwick, Noah. *The Evolution of a State, or Recollections of Old Texas Days*. Austin: University of Texas Press, 1983.

"Social Life in Early Texas." Daughters of the Republic of Texas Library at the Alamo, San Antonio.

Standard Dictionary of Folklore Mythology and Legend. New York: Funk & Wagnalls, 1949.

"Stars behind the Country Music Explosion." *San Antonio Express-News*, November 23, 1980.

Stovall, Allan A. *Nueces Headwater Country*. San Antonio: Naylor Co., 1959.

Stumpf, Mrs. Franz. "San Antonio's Menger." San Antonio, 1953.

Sullivan, Dulcie. "Celebration." *Cattleman*. November 1960.

Texas Writer's Project (1850–1898). Work Projects Administration, Austin Copy, Dist. 9, W.P. 16206, CP 185-1-66-109. Austin, Texas, Public Library, History Center.

"They Came from 50 Miles Around and Danced from Sun to Sun." *The XIT Brand Annual*. Dalhart, Tex., 1939.

Thompson, Taylor. "Reminiscences of Early Day Social Life on Texas Frontiers." 1963. Daughters of the Republic of Texas Library at the Alamo, San Antonio.

Timmons, Carolyn and Herbert. ". . . and the dance went on." *Cattleman*. July 1963.

Townsend, Charles R. *San Antonio Rose: The Life and Music of Bob Wills*. Urbana: University of Illinois Press, 1976.

Trager, James, ed. *The People's Chronology*. New York: Holt, Rinehart & Winston, 1979.

Turner, Martha Ann. *Old Nacogdoches in the Jazz Age*. Austin: Madrona Press, 1976.

Webb, Walter Prescott. "Christmas and New Year in Texas." *Southwestern Historical Quarterly* 44 (July 1940–April 1941).

Whatley, Mary Clark. *The Swenson Saga*. Austin: Jenkins Publishing Co., 1976.

White, Betty. *Betty White's Teen-Age Dance Book*. New York: Pocket Books, 1962.

Whitlock, V. H. *Cowboy Life on the Llano Estacado*. Norman: University of Oklahoma Press, 1970.

Williams, Jill. "Keeping Fit to a Fiddle." *Saturday Evening Post*. October 1981.

Wright, Anita Peters, and Dexter Wright. *How to Dance*. New York: Perma Giants, 1949.

Index